719.95

THE SOUTH WALES MAIN LINE

PART ONE
CARDIFF

BY

JOHN HODGE

Featuring the photographs of John Hodge and R.O. Tuck.

The main passenger train building at Cardiff General in the early 1960s, located on the north side of the station site. The photograph was taken from the top of Marland House, which housed the Cardiff District and Divisional Offices from 1960; its flat roof offered an excellent vantage point for the station forecourt and the bus station.

WILD SWAN PUBLICATIONS

Designed by Paul Karau
Printed by Amadeus Press, Cleckheaton

Published by
WILD SWAN PUBLICATIONS LTD.
1-3 Hagbourne Road, Didcot, Oxon, OX11 8DP

DEDICATION

It gives me great pleasure to dedicate this book to the former Cardiff Canton Shedmaster W. W. (Bill) Wagstaff and his Shift Foremen Charlie Hewlett and Ivor Hockey, with grateful thanks for their good offices in allowing me (and Bob Tuck) open access to the depot for photography, and also for making available to me engine diagrams and depot record books. I spent many happy hours in the shed office, especially when Ivor was on duty, observing the general operation of the shed, and enjoying the wealth of experiences and good humour which never failed to emanate from drivers, firemen and shed staff alike.

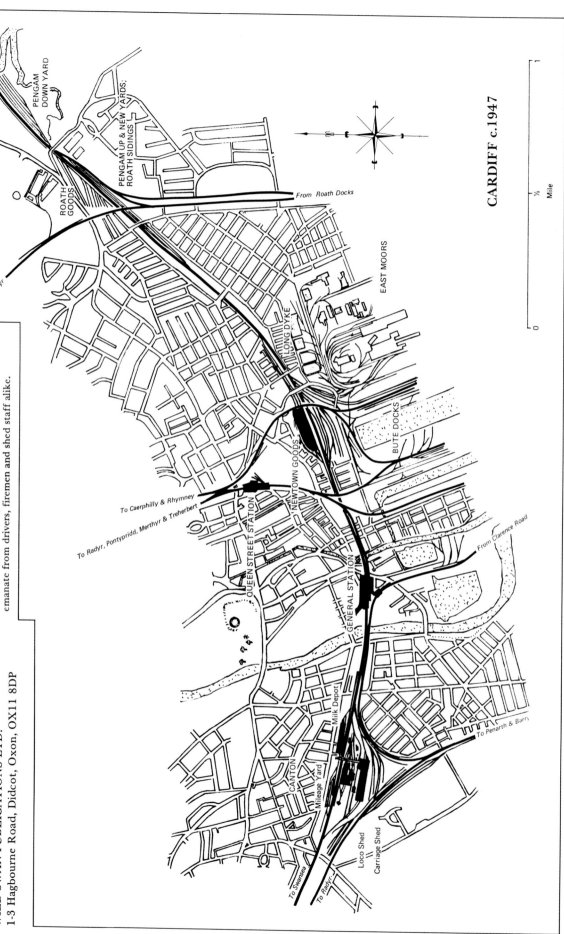

CARDIFF c.1947

PREFACE

Rugby internationals at Cardiff Arms Park produced huge crowds of supporters, many of whom travelled by special trains, especially from points west of Cardiff. Specials from the Neath, Swansea, Llanelly and Carmarthen areas would often start from the Valley stations in those districts, and produced a succession of 'A' headcode trains hauled mainly by Landore 'Castles', Llanelly 'Granges' and Standard 'Class 5s', and Carmarthen 'Castles'. Rather than stable the trains at Canton – which would have caused heavy occupation at Cardiff West and problems at the carriage shed sidings – the trains ran forward empty to Pengam Yard; here, the sidings had been mostly cleared of freight stock for the day to provide accommodation for the special trains. Engines were grouped together and sent to Canton for servicing, returning in mid-afternoon to stand with their trains. Passenger Train Inspectors Ted Kibblewhite and Tom Meyrick shared the supervision at the yard to ensure smooth working, and one of these gentlemen can be seen in the four-foot. Eight specials can be seen in this view of Pengam Down yard on Saturday, 11th March 1961 awaiting departure. The trains were facing Cardiff General station, two miles to the west, and are numbered in the sequence 'Z17' to 'Z24'.

As a native of South Wales who grew up with close associations with Cardiff, I witnessed the final years of Cardiff's greatness in the steam era, from 1949 onwards. Having a great interest in operating, I gained access to the Cardiff Canton Shed Office from the mid 1950s, where I studied all the engine record books, diagrams, etc., and had free access to the depot for photography. In 1954, I met R.O. (Bob) Tuck, who had recently moved to Cardiff from Lincoln, and he and I took many photographs of railway activities in Cardiff and the surrounding area, which form the basis of this book. In the early 1950s, I used an Ensign 16 on 120 camera, and in January 1957 bought a Voigtlander Vito II 35mm camera, which I used exclusively until the early 1960s, when I bought a Rolleiflex. Bob Tuck throughout the period used a Voigtlander Bessa II, which gave 8 exposures on 120 film. Bob is now in his 90th year and is still active with a Pentax 35mm camera, recording the current diesel scene.

I owe much of my knowledge of the Cardiff locomotive scene to the good services of the Canton shedmaster and his shed foremen during the latter part of the 1950s and early 1960s, before the shed closed in September 1962 for conversion to a diesel depot, with removal of everything to Cardiff East Dock. The Shedmaster was W. W. (Bill) Wagstaff, and the Shift Foremen Charlie Hewlett and Ivor Hockey. The Shedmaster was typical of similar men of his era; he was a long-term locoman who had started out firing on the Fishguard boat trains with the many 'Saints' allocated to Canton at that time. He had a strict, no-nonsense approach to the job, reflecting the responsibility vested in him, but was happy to accept Bob Tuck and me into the depot, and sometimes attended local railway society meetings with us. Charlie Hewlett was widely known by train crews all over South Wales, having previously worked at Pontypool Road and Barry depots. To those who greeted him with a 'How are you, Charlie?', he would invariably reply 'Never Better!' and those readers who remember him and his constant good humour will be pleased to see a photograph including him on page 90. I received much help and information from Ivor Hockey, whom I am delighted to include in the dedication of this book. Invariably sitting at his desk with his trilby hat on, he was the most affable of persons, never flapped, and must have been a huge credit to the working of the depot.

For photographers, Cardiff was a poor place for good vantage points. Perhaps this was one reason why there had been a dearth of railway photographers recording the scene at Cardiff prior to the early 1950s when Sid Rickard, Bob Tuck, Alan Jarvis and I became active. Prior to this, only H.L. Hopwood, in the first three decades, had done much in the way of photography, largely on an engine-only basis. Other than F.K. (Ken) Davies of Neath, who visited Cardiff from time to time from the mid-1930s, and J.G. Hubback who photographed mostly in the countryside between Cardiff and Bridgend, Cardiff had been very under-photographed until the 1950s. Good vantage points existed only from Pengam Bridge in the east and Canton Bridge in the west. The station, with its long equal-length main line platforms and curves at either end, offered little scope for interesting shots, though this was made up for by the sight of the resplendent 'Castles', 'Britannias' and 'Kings' which came up from Canton and stood in the middle road waiting to take on the next London express. Through my friendship with the various Assistant Station Masters, especially John Hall in the early '60s, I gained access to the East and West boxes for photographic purposes, and was able to have a limited access to the track, at the signalmen's discretion.

The photographs included in this volume are from the 1950s, especially the latter half, and the early 1960s. The intention is to portray the still heavy steam operation, when only diesel shunters and the Blue Pullman represented the impending alternative form of traction soon to become dominant. I hope that these pictures of the Cardiff scene will bring back many happy memories to those who, like me, knew them so well, and show younger readers what they missed!

John Hodge

No.4079 *Pendennis Castle* pausing at Marshfield station with a down local passenger train on Sunday, 14th October 1951, possibly the 1.15 p.m. Gloucester to Cardiff. Marshfield was the only intermediate station in the twelve miles between Newport and Cardiff, and served the adjacent village of that name. There was also a station at Roath, about 1¼ miles east of Cardiff General, until wartime closure in 1917. No.4079 was transferred to Gloucester in November 1948, moving on to Stafford Road in October 1952.

EASTERN APPROACHES

'Grange' 4-6-0 No.6872 *Crawley Grange* passing through Marshfield station with the 10.20 a.m. (SO) Penzance to Swansea on 30th July 1955. This train was diagrammed for a through engine from Plymouth, but by its departure at 1.25 p.m., the best motive power available on Laira shed had invariably been utilised. Despite the long working, the crew could never be sure of a suitable engine, and although a 'Hall' or a 'Grange' was the more likely, anything from a '43XX' to a 'Castle' might be supplied.

It is 150 years since the South Wales Railway opened its 75-mile broad gauge line from Chepstow to Newport, Cardiff and Swansea in June 1850. During that time, the line grew to become one of the busiest and most important sections of line in the country, serving the ever-expanding South Wales industrial scene, dominated by the coal, iron and steel industries, and by the docks. Cardiff initially faced compatibility problems with gauge, as the Taff Vale and Rhymney Railways were both to the 'narrow' 4ft 8½in gauge, whereas the South Wales Railway was to the 7ft. This problem continued until 1872, when the Great Western Railway, which had absorbed its South Wales Railway in 1863, converted the whole of its South Wales system to the 'standard' gauge.

Passenger services through Cardiff by 1876 were modest by later standards, with three fast trains and a late mail each way between New Milford and Paddington (via Gloucester), with a similar number of other, slower through services to Gloucester or Paddington, a few of which conveyed additional through coaches. At best, the down journey took just under 5 hours, and the up 5¼. There were four services each way to Hereford, and four more to Portskewett (for the New Passage ferry, and trains thence to Bristol), together with a handful of local services. Fast services improved considerably with the opening of the Severn Tunnel ten years later, and times of 4hrs 3 mins were scheduled to and from Paddington (via Bath and the tunnel) in each direction soon afterwards. As a rapidly-expanding city and important business centre, Cardiff was now receiving a service more in keeping with its standing in the country.

Goods services included the fast 'Irish Goods' each way between London and New Milford, goods to Gloucester, Bristol and Birmingham, coal to Swindon (transfer) and Brentford, and a number of more local workings. By the end of the 19th century, Cardiff was the leading port in the country, thanks to the vast quantities of coal shipped abroad. With its Coal Exchange at Bute Docks controlling the purchase and movement of coal to all parts of the globe, Cardiff became the coal capital of the world; the black gold made vast fortunes for pit owners, coal factors, railway and dock owners, and shippers alike. Coal export reached its peak in 1913, with Cardiff Docks dispatching around 10½ million tons in that year, and nearby Penarth another 4 million, the total coal production in South Wales being around 56 million tons.

A further improvement of passenger services from London occurred in 1903 with the completion of the Badminton cut-off. The fastest journey from Cardiff to London in 1906 was 2hrs 40 mins, and 2hrs 55 mins in the down direction, with eight- or nine-coach trains. From 1903, engine changing on London expresses, which had previously been carried out at Newport, was transferred to Cardiff.

Over the years, various facilities at Cardiff had often been improved, especially in 1896, but the modifications carried out in the early 1930s were most significant. Although the trade depression at the beginning of the 1930s had a radical effect on South Wales, the Great Western Board nevertheless approved a massive plan for upgrading the line through Cardiff between 1931-4. With an old and restrictive layout, and out-of-date signalling, Cardiff General was completely rebuilt and remodelled, with a new track layout and signalling throughout between Newtown West and Leckwith Junction.

Cardiff had increased in size tenfold (to around 225,000) in the eighty years since the arrival of the railway, and the modifications were vital to the further development of not only the city, but also the large Valleys catchment area. The new arrangements served Cardiff well until (and beyond) the steam era.

The main express passenger service had established at six down and seven up trains from and to Paddington, with additional services on Saturdays and at peak traffic periods. Cardiff had also seen the development of a considerable number of cross-country services, and in 1935, daily trains to Paignton, Portsmouth, Brighton, Birmingham, Birkenhead, Manchester, Liverpool and Newcastle-upon-Tyne were running from the city.

Coal production in South Wales and Monmouthshire had fallen considerably since the First World War, and by 1946 was down to 20 million tons. Cardiff's export of coal fell even more sharply, with just over a million tons being shipped in that year. Although the age of coal was passing, other industrial and commercial functions (e.g. iron, steel and oil traffics) took its place, and Cardiff maintained its importance within the railway system. Coal shipment finally ceased at Cardiff Docks in 1963, when all export and coastwise traffic from East Wales was concentrated at Barry Docks.

Heavy freight engines were a not-uncommon sight on passenger-rated services in South Wales during the latter 1950s. This view shows '28XX' class 2-8-o No.3823 moving across from Up Main to Up Relief with an empty stock train on Saturday, 2nd August 1958, comprising Southern Region vehicles. This had probably worked to Cardiff earlier that day, and was being returned to its home system, probably via Salisbury. On the right can be seen the edge of St. Mellons Stores Depot (originally Ministry of Works & Transport), which was served by a rail complex.

Marshfield had a milk depot that received supplies from local farms for conveyance to London. Tanks from the depot were worked to Cardiff in mid-afternoon to connect with whichever of the Whitland milk trains had capacity on the day, and No.6116 is seen here on Canton target 'H14' with a train of five tanks (carrying up to 15,000 gallons of milk) heading for Cardiff. The '61XX' class was, until 1950, to be found more or less entirely at London division sheds, though examples had been temporarily attached further afield – to the West Country in 1941/2, for instance. From 1950, a few of the engines were to be found in Bristol, and from 1953 also in the Wolverhampton and Newport divisions.

'Manor' No.7823 *Hook Norton Manor* clearing St. Mellons West with a westbound return excursion on Thursday, 14th June 1956, with ex-Great Western stock dominant. The engine still had a Croes Newydd (84J) shed plate on the smokebox door, despite the fact that she had been transferred to Cornwall during the previous December. Although nominally shedded at Truro at this time, 7823 was recorded as being briefly allocated to Neath during June/July 1956, probably for such excursion work, returning to Truro afterwards.

'Britannia' No.70024 *Vulcan* passing St. Mellons West on Tuesday, 9th May 1961, with the down 'Capitals Limited Express'. The title was bestowed on the 8.0 a.m. Cardiff to Paddington and the 3.55 p.m. Paddington to Cardiff services in 1956. During the spring of 1961, *Vulcan* was used consistently on London duties during a controlled period of operation, mostly involving the 10.0 a.m. Cardiff to Paddington, the 3.55 p.m. return through to Swansea, and the 1.8 a.m. parcels back to Cardiff, the longest running between coaling (at Landore) on the Western Region, some 340 miles in total. The Canton crew on the footplate would be relieved at Cardiff General.

Radyr shed had several of the '72XX' class 2-8-2Ts, which were utilised on the longer-distance main-line freights, including regular workings to Severn Tunnel Jct. and Salisbury. No.7202 is seen here on Thursday, 14th June 1956, with the down '406' duty, covering the 1.15 p.m. Radyr Quarry to Severn Tunnel Jct., and the 4.20 p.m. Severn Tunnel to Penarth Curve trains.

The 9.15 a.m. Manchester (London Road) to Swansea was worked through to Pontypool Road by a Longsight 'Patriot', 'Jubilee' or 'Royal Scot', with a further engine change at Cardiff. Pontypool Road sometimes turned out a '41XX' class 2-6-2T for the run to Cardiff, but on Saturday, 3rd August 1957, a Barry '56XX' 0-6-2T No. 5614 was used, and is seen here at St. Mellons West. This engine had replaced a failed Pontypool Road '41XX' at Barry the previous weekend on a return excursion from Barry Island to Pontypool Road. The '41XX' at Barry was returned light to Cardiff, and on the 4.40 p.m. Cardiff to Manchester as far as Pontypool Road. Thus, both engines were returned to their home sheds. A mixture of ex-GW and LMS stock is evident in the train.

WD 'Austerity' 2-8-0 No.90573 from Canton with a down 'H' class freight at St. Mellons on Tuesday, 16th May 1961. The 'Austerities' were a familiar sight in South Wales, though with large numbers of ex-GW eight-coupled engines still available, they were not as numerous as on some other regions. There were around twenty of the engines at Newport Division sheds in the mid-1950s, with examples at Ebbw Jct, Canton and Pontypool Road.

Landore 'Hall' No.5929 *Hanham Hall* with the 4.2 p.m. Gloucester to Cardiff service approaching Rumney River Bridge Jct. c.1958. The four-coach 'classic' rake of Van Third, Third, Compo and Van Third, was a combination to be found not only as a single train, but also within longer express services as a through portion.

Summer Saturdays in the 1950s invariably saw '43XX' class 2-6-0s being utilised on secondary expresses, especially on services to and from the Southern Region. Canton '43' No.6352 is seen here at Rumney River Bridge with the nine-coach 9.20 a.m. Swansea to Bournemouth (Train No.780) on Saturday, 2nd August 1958. The engine was scheduled to work this train through to Salisbury, returning to Bristol later that evening, and on to Cardiff the following day. An LMR van can be seen leading the formation.

Canton's top passenger turn of the day was the up 'Red Dragon' (10.0 a.m. Cardiff) and the down 'Capitals United' (3.55 p.m. Paddington). Canton's newly acquired 'Castle' No.4080 *Powderham Castle* is pictured at Rumney River Bridge with 'The Red Dragon', 7.30 a.m. Carmarthen to Paddington, on 17th August 1960, a fortnight after her arrival. The full brake vehicle provided at the head of the train was to give sufficient luggage or mail capacity, with BR Mk I stock forming the majority of the train. After a 'Heavy Intermediate' repair at Swindon, No.4080 was transferred to Newton Abbot in April of that year for a short spell, then on to Shrewsbury until August; on arrival at Canton, she was acclaimed as an excellent addition to the 'class 7' fleet. This view shows No.4080 overtaking '94XX' 0-6-0T No.8470 on an up coal train.

The up 'South Wales Pullman', 4.35 p.m. Swansea, accelerating away from Cardiff past Rumney River Bridge behind Landore 'Castle' No. 5080 *Defiant* on Thursday, 6th June 1957. The Great Western had experimented with the use of Pullman trains on regular and special services in 1929/30, but their use was not deemed to be a success. They were reintroduced on this train in the summer of 1955, formed of First Class Parlour or Kitchen Cars, a Bar/Kitchen Car, and Second Class Parlour or Kitchen Cars, sandwiched between Second Class Brake coaches. There was an 8s (first class) or 4s 6d (second class) supplement for a single journey on top of the normal fare between Cardiff and London (first single, 34s 5d; second single 22s 11d).

There were never many four-coupled tank engines allocated to industrial South Wales; in the late 1930s, only Llantrisant, Merthyr, Newport and Pontypool Road had a regular presence. By the latter half of the 1950s, only a couple of four-coupled tank engines were to be found, at Llantrisant (for Penygraig branch work) and Newport, and these had gone by 1958. Here No.1421 from Newport (Ebbw Jct.) shed was making her way home on Thursday, 6th June 1957, with the 6.5 p.m. Cardiff to Newport three-coach local train, just to the east of Rumney River Bridge Jct., the signal box for which is silhouetted against Connies & Meaden's steel works.

As so often happened, the relief portion of 'The Red Dragon', 9.45 a.m. from Cardiff, was worked by a 'Hall', which doubtless had some difficulty in keeping ahead of the main train with 'class 7' power behind it. Nevertheless, the 15-minute separation of the trains was expected to be maintained all the way to Paddington. In this instance, Canton 'Hall' No.5925 *Eastcote Hall* is shown passing Rumney River Bridge with the 9.45 a.m. Cardiff relief express of around 12 coaches on Wednesday, 9th April 1958. Ex-private owner wagons were interspersed with steel mineral types in Rumney Sidings, on the left.

'Britannias' appeared on Western Region services during 1951, based at Old Oak and Laira. In late 1952, Nos.70025-29 were allocated to Canton, and their extensive use on the London trains began. From January 1957, the full complement of 15 Western Region 'Britannias' were concentrated at Canton, who used its latest ex-works examples and few remaining 'Castles' for the main duties to London – 8.0 a.m., 10.0 a.m. and 12.0 noon from Cardiff. No.70022 *Tornado* is seen here on the Up Main with the Paddington-bound 'The Red Dragon' (10.0 a.m. Cardiff) on Wednesday, 9th April 1958. 'The Red Dragon' was normally formed of six coaches from Carmarthen, two from Swansea, and five (including a dining pair) from Cardiff at the rear, with an additional vehicle on Mondays, Fridays and Saturdays. The stock carried the chocolate and cream livery, introduced in the latter 1950s for the Western Region's named express services.

Double-heading was not often seen in this part of South Wales during this period, and then mostly as a means of positioning a locomotive by avoiding light engine mileage. This picture shows the very last 'Star', No.4056 *Princess Margaret* (Bath Road shed), and '43XX' class 2-6-0 No.6370 (Canton) heading eastwards with the 7.5 p.m. Cardiff to Bristol service on Friday, 26th July 1957. The 'Star' was on a Cardiff diagram that worked the overnight Cardiff to Plymouth parcels onwards from Temple Meads, returning the following day with the 7.50 a.m. Newquay to Manchester train from Plymouth to Pontypool Road, and thence with the 7.10 p.m. Manchester to Cardiff. Cardiff & Bristol local services ran roughly at 2-hour intervals throughout the day, supplemented by through expresses to and from the South and West of England, which ran fast between Newport and Bristol.

A considerable amount of milk traffic was worked from South Wales to the various dairies in West and South London, with Kensington and Wood Lane the main destinations. Three of the daily trains at this time originated at Whitland, and a fourth at Carmarthen, though additional tanks were conveyed from locations further east. These trains called at or passed through Cardiff between about 7.20 p.m. and 12.40 a.m. each night. Due to the perishable nature of the liquid, and the weight of the train (each full tank weighing around 28 tons), 'Castles' were generally provided on the services. No.5038 *Morlais Castle*, from Old Oak shed, is seen here with the 3.50 p.m. Whitland to Kensington on Thursday, 6th June 1957, the train containing both conventional and rotank (road-rail) vehicles, with the usual passenger brake at the rear. This was a Swindon turn off the 1.0 a.m. Paddington to Swansea, for which Swindon sometimes used an ex-works locomotive, as here.

Pengam Down Yard was situated on the eastern outskirts of the city, with 17 sidings stop-blocked at the Rumney River Bridge (eastern) end. Trains had therefore to be shunted into or out of the yard via the goods reception roads, and the headshunt on the Docks branch, immediately to the west. Having attached its brake van, Canton '43XX' class 2-6-0 No.6352 is seen heading out of the Down Goods Loop at Pengam Yard with an 'F' class freight to West Wales.

PENGAM & ROATH

The 9.25 a.m. Manchester to Swansea service passing Pengam Yard on Saturday, 29th June 1957 behind '51XX' class 2-6-2T No.4138, from Pontypool Road shed. '51XX' class engines were rated as similar to the 'Manors' and '43XXs', and a 12-coach train was well within their capabilities on the favourable gradients from Pontypool Road. The train was formed mostly of ex-LMS stock on this occasion.

By the end of the 19th century, the increasing volume of traffic and marshalling requirements at Newtown and Long Dyke led to the opening of Pengam Yard, on the eastern outskirts of Cardiff, in 1898. Because of the proximity of the Rhymney River in one direction and the planned position of the Roath Dock Branch in the other, it was not possible to make the yard double-ended. Pengam Down Yard of 17 sidings was fully stop-blocked towards the west, involving use of a headshunt on the Roath Branch when necessary to reverse into the yard.

For eastbound starting trains, an Up Yard of seven sidings, stop-blocked at the west end, was created to the west of Pengam Junction Signal Box. Directly west of this were a further six sidings named New Yard with five being stop-blocked, again at the west end, and one being a through road into Roath Sidings, another yard of six sidings again located directly to the west, with one through road from New Yard and the others stop-blocked at the east end.

To the west of the new Pengam Yard, but on the up side, 1901 saw the opening of Roath Goods Yard, with Roath (Newport Road) Coal Yard opened in 1909. The Roath Docks Branch from Pengam Jct. opened in 1903.

In later years, the existence of so many small marshalling yards created a fragmented and confusing position for the overall marshalling scene for Cardiff, and there were constant efforts at rationalisation. In addition to the yards along the main line, huge areas of sidings existed on the docks, especially at Tidal and Marshalling Sidings, originally laid in for shipment coal, but increasingly used for more general traffic in later years. When Pengam Yard was required for the building of the Cardiff Freightliner Depot, all marshalling ceased there in November 1966 and was largely transferred to Tidal Sidings, with the new depot opening in June 1967. At the same time, Pengam Up Yard, New Yard and Roath Sidings were all taken out of use and recovered, leaving only the Pengam Freightliner Depot. This is now to be replaced by a new and larger Freightliner depot near St. Mellons, which can (at last) be served by a through yard.

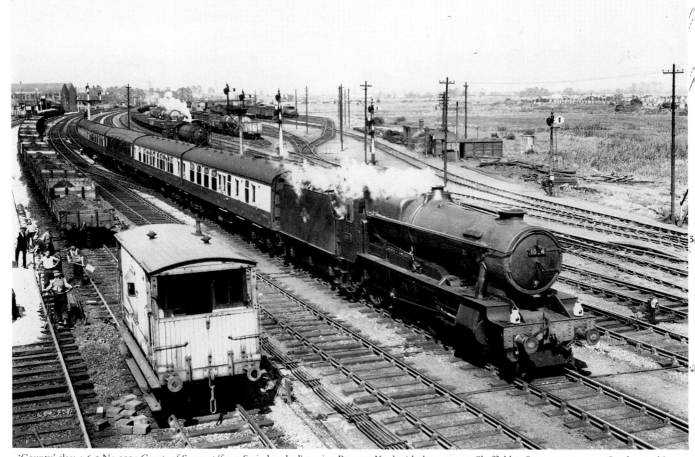

'County' class 4-6-0 No.1004 *County of Somerset* (from Swindon shed) passing Pengam Yard with the 9.20 a.m. Sheffield to Swansea express on Sunday, 2nd June 1957, as relaying was proceeding on one of the up loops. This Sunday train, together with its balancing up service, the 10.55 a.m. Swansea, was introduced by the Great Western and Great Central companies in 1921 as a supplemental provision to the weekday Swansea & Newcastle through trains. Running via Banbury and Didcot (West Curve), the train took eight hours for the 285 miles, with the luxury of a buffet car between Swindon and Swansea during the summer months. An unusual aspect of this service was that it was worked through from Sheffield to Swindon by Eastern Region locomotives - usually 'B1' 4-6-0s - which returned to ER metals with the balancing Sunday train. Included in the formation were a couple of ex-LNER coaches.

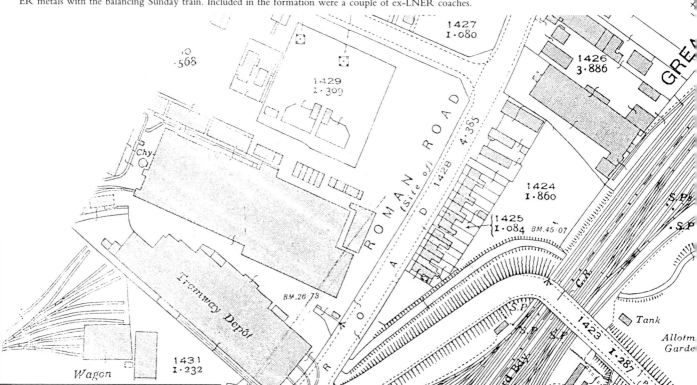

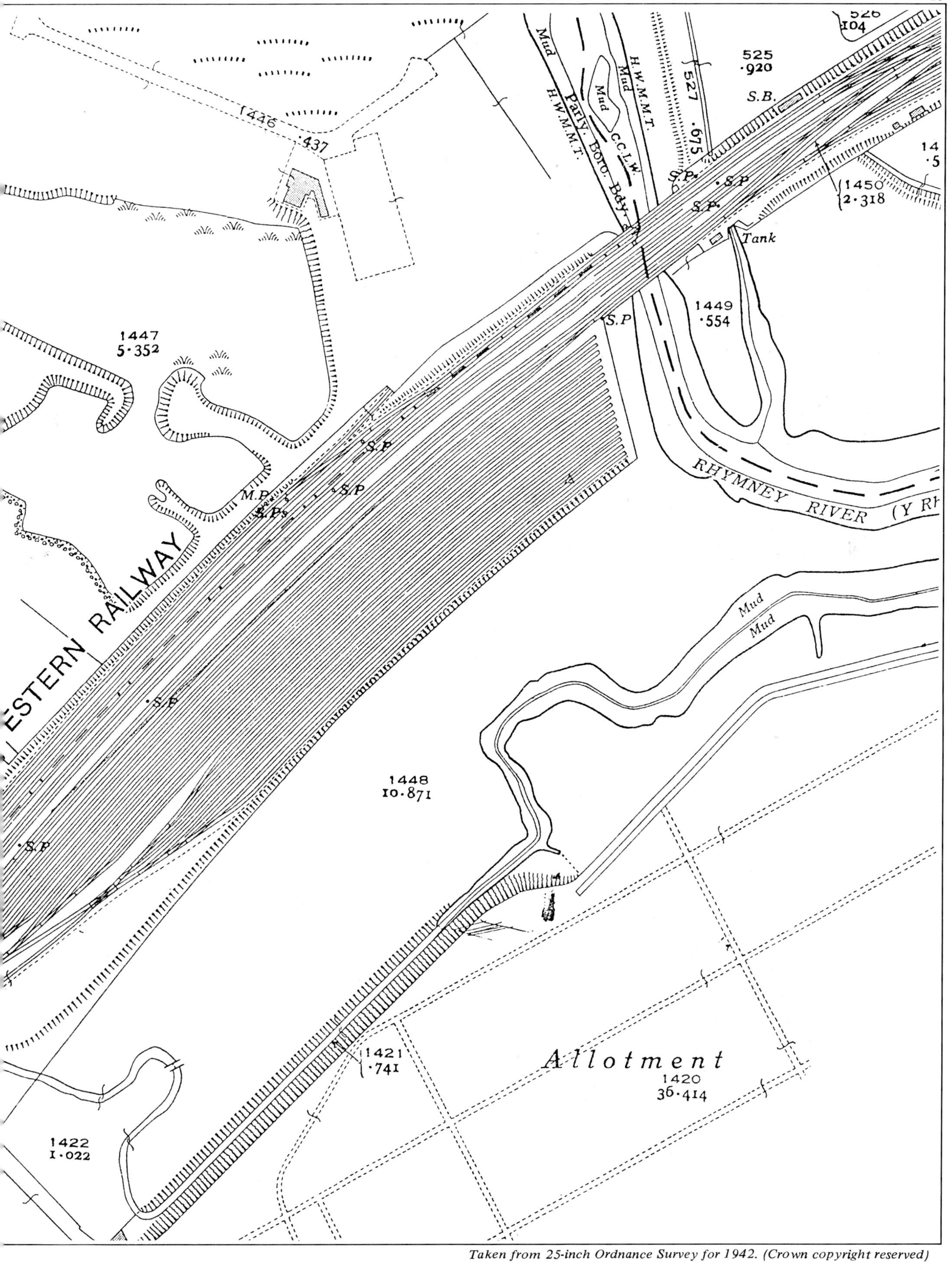

526
104
525
·920
S.B.
527
·675
Mud
H.W.M.M.T.
Mud
Mud
Parly. Boro. Bdy.
C.C.L.W.
H.W.M.M.T.
1446
·437
S.P.
S.P
S.P.
1450
2·318
14
·5
Tank
1449
·554
S.P
1447
5·352
S.P
S.P
M.P.
S.Ps
RHYMNEY RIVER (Y RH
ESTERN RAILWAY
Mud
Mud
S.P
1448
10·871
S.P
1421
·741
Allotment
1420
36·414
1422
1·022

Taken from 25-inch Ordnance Survey for 1942. (Crown copyright reserved)

The 7.55 a.m. Paddington to Swansea and Milford Haven was a fairly light service, with the leading two vehicles for Milford, and the remainder from the Dining Car destined for Swansea. Old Oak usually provided motive power, and that shed's 'Hall' class No.5941 *Campion Hall* is seen here skirting Pengam Yard on Tuesday, 8th August 1958 with the train. The service was running on the Down Main at this point, with the Up Main and Up Goods (on which the long, up coal train can be seen) to its left, and the Up and Down Relief lines to its right. The siding to the left of the goods train was that from which the private sidings to the Schweppes (mineral waters), Lewis (agricultural machinery) and Connies & Meaden (steel) companies were served.

Tyseley's well-kept 'Modified Halls' worked regularly to Cardiff with through services from Birmingham. Here, No.6971 *Athelhampton Hall* was passing Pengam Down Yard with the 3.45 p.m. Snow Hill to Fishguard Harbour on Saturday, 19th July 1958, having run via Stratford-on-Avon and Gloucester. There were a considerable number of trains running between the two cities daily during the summer months, with around five via the North Warwicks line, and six via Worcester and Hereford. The lead into Schweppes private siding from the first up loop can be clearly seen.

'Castle', No.4073 *Caerphilly Castle* (Canton) moving across from the Up Main to the Up Relief at Pengam Jct. with the Sunday 4.45 p.m. Cardiff to Paddington, on 2nd June 1957. The train was a scheduled thirteen-coach set without a dining car, due into Paddington at 8.5 p.m. Those travellers wishing to dine were directed onto the following train, the 12.25 p.m. Milford Haven, which left Cardiff at 5.0 p.m. and conveyed a Composite Dining Saloon and a Kitchen Buffet Car pair.

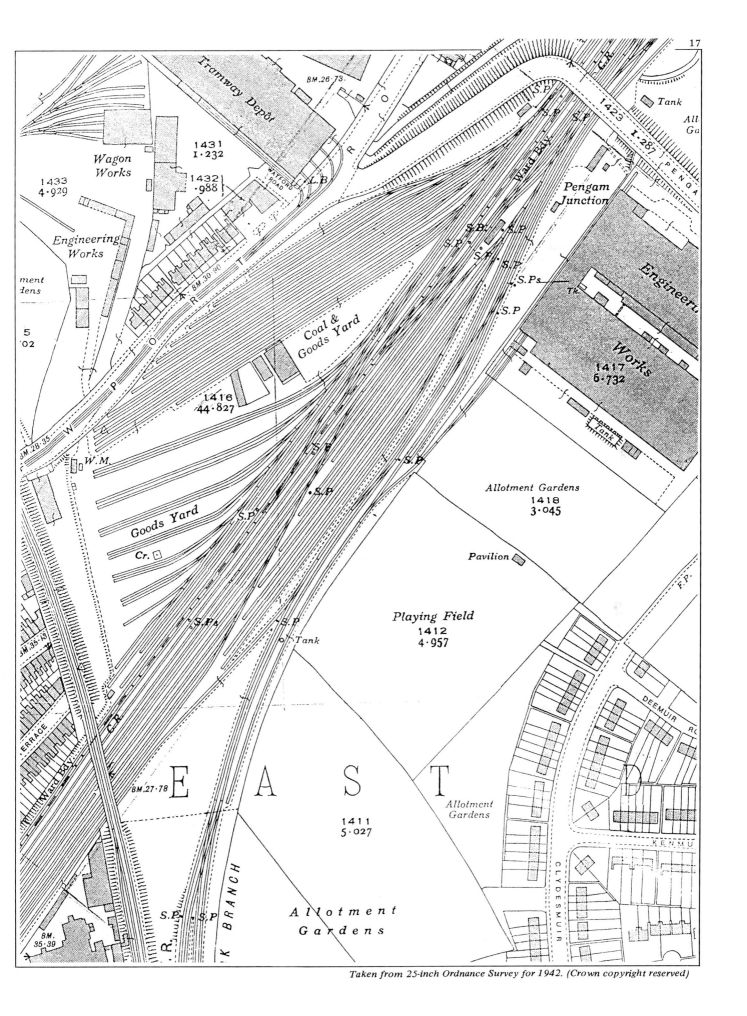

Pengam Up Yard (also known locally as 'Back of the Box Sidings') and Roath Up side Coal and Mileage Yards were adjacent to one another, overlooked by Pengam bridge, the road over which ran from Newport Road to Pengam Moors airfield and environs, and provided an excellent vantage point. 'King' No.6028 *King George VI*, is seen passing Pengam Jct signal box with the 7.20 p.m. Cardiff to Pontypool Road Mail to connect at the latter point with the 12.0 noon Penzance to Manchester, which included through vehicles to Glasgow. The leading TPO sorting vehicle ran from Cardiff to Liverpool, and was attached to the Penzance at Pontypool Road; for many years, the vehicles involved were Sorting Carriages Nos.801, 802 or 803, introduced onto the service when new in 1934. This view was taken on Wednesday, 13th June 1962, during the final months of 'King' operations from Canton. An ex-gunpowder van with flush doors can be seen towards the rear of the goods train on the left.

'72XX' class 2-8-2T No.7236 passing Roath Mileage Yard with a class 'H' Margam to Severn Tunnel Jct. freight, comprising a pair of oil tanks for Avonmouth at the head of merchandise and mineral open wagons. The train was running on the Up Relief with a clear road ahead, on the sunny morning of Tuesday, 8th April 1958. '56XX' No.6693 from Pontypool Road features behind the '72' on the Down Goods line.

Even when there was no traffic on the running lines, there was always plenty of activity to be seen from Pengam bridge with shunting of the various yards. To the north of the running lines at Pengam Jct. were the mileage yards and storage sidings, and Newport Road coal yard. In Great Western days, the sidings next to the mileage yard were specified in the *Appendix to the Service Timetable* for traffic worked to Pengam to relieve Newtown Goods. In the 1950s and 60s, there were also warehouses situated between the coal sidings and the remainder of the yard, and full wagonloads were accepted for offloading by the firms' staff. By the late 1950s, no specific through trains served the up side sidings, and they were worked by trip engines from other yards. '94XX' class 0-6-0PT No.3408 is seen on the 'Y5' duty, the 7.20 a.m. Radyr Quarry Jct. to Pengam Sidings, on 8th April 1958, with two single bolster wagons at the near end. The shunters alongside the cab were discussing the next move with the driver, while a '56XX' and a '43XX' were waiting on the Up Goods loop.

A down iron ore train from Banbury taking the Down Loop line alongside the Roath Docks branch at Pengam Jct. box behind Canton 'Austerity' class 2–8–0 No.90148 on Monday, 20th July 1959. This particular load was destined for Guest, Keen & Nettlefolds' East Moors (Dowlais Works) steelworks, a massive site located in the north-east section of the docks and industrial area. The 'Austerity' engines first appeared on the Great Western on loan in 1944, and again in 1946/7, becoming part of the nationalised concern in 1948. By 1951, there were around a hundred of the class allocated to the Western Region, but four years later, less than half of that number remained.

'56XX' class 0–6–2T No.6637 from Barry shed passing Pengam Jct. on Monday, 20th July 1959, with a five-coach up special (X02) of ex-GW stock, probably from the Barry line. The passengers were no doubt experiencing a good shaking with the fore-and-aft movement of these engines when travelling at speed. Pengam Up and New Yards can be seen behind the coaches, and beyond the bridge in the background, Roath Sidings. Pengam sidings in Great Western days were specified in the *Appendix* for empty wagons from the dock lines destined for the Newport District Eastern and Western Valley lines, or freight for destinations on those lines.

Target 'Z1' signified the 9.35 a.m. Llantrisant duty, on which '42XX' No.4273 from Cwm Ovens on Tuesday, 8th April 1958. The train was crossing between the Up Main and the Up Goods Loop at Pengam Jct., doubtless in preparation for work in one of the yards. Whilst a number of steel mineral wagons were at the head of the train, most of the remainder seem to have been of various wooden designs. As coke traffic was light in weight, wooden wagons had their sides extended upwards in order to carry a greater load, and several such vehicles can be seen in this train. A good view of the dozen or so Roath storage sidings is afforded here, with the Roath Mileage to their left, in the distance.

A pannier tank heading a mixed train for the docks area along the Roath Docks branch on 20th July 1959, with loads for which Guest, Keens were probably the main recipient. In addition to coal and other traffic for shipment, many other items were conveyed into the complex, which incorporated a large number of industrial concerns handling metals, timber, etc. The connections between the Main, Relief and Roath Docks lines may be clearly seen in this view.

The last steam engine to be constructed at Swindon was BR Standard '9F' 2-10-0 No.92220 *Evening Star*, seen here coming off the Roath Docks branch on Wednesday, 30th May 1962, with the 6.10 p.m. Cardiff Docks to Soho Pool (Birmingham) Regent oil tanks. The engine was scheduled to return with the 9.20 p.m. Soho the following evening. Oil was particularly handled in the docks from around the Second World War, with the Gulf Oil company latterly involved. The working of No.92220, while based at Canton, had to be closely controlled to ensure that she returned home regularly for cleaning and maintenance in view of the special workings and exhibitions for which the engine was required.

Another Swindon-built locomotive was LMS '8F' No.48450, crossing from the Up Main to the Relief at Pengam Jct. on 30th May 1962 with a class 'D' ('5') express freight comprised of vans. Constructed between 1943 and 1945, the eighty engines (8400-79) worked on the Great Western until 1946/7, when they were transferred onto the LMS. No.48450 carried the BR shed code 84F, Stourbridge Jct. To her left, '28XX' No.3860 can be seen emerging from Roath Up sidings onto the Roath Docks branch with some open and bogie bolster wagons. The nest of sidings to the west of the signal box was Pengam Up Yard; along with New Yard and Roath Sidings beyond, nearly all were stop-blocked.

The low sun was highlighting this up class 'C' ('4') vacuum express freight as it passed Pengam Jct. box during the evening of 20th July 1959. The train was hauled by Newport (Ebbw Jct.) 4-6-0 No.6838 *Goodmoor Grange*, which, along with about thirty other engines of its class, retained a 3,500-gallon tender at this time. The 'vacs' at this time were comprised mostly of vans and opens, many of the latter running sheeted.

No.2899 leaving Pengam Up Yard during the evening of Saturday, 6th May 1961, with a breakdown train, carrying the designated 'B' headlamps of a service 'NOT going to clear the line'; 'A' lamps were carried when the train was heading for the scene of an incident. The Great Western purchased large steam breakdown cranes mostly from Cowan Sheldon, though such companies as Ransomes & Rapier and Stothart & Pitt also supplied them. In the early 1930s, two 35T Cowan cranes were stationed in the Cardiff area - No.9 at Caerphilly and No.10 at Cathays; in the 1950s, breakdown gangs were shown as operating from Canton and Cathays, and by the end of the 1950s Canton had the latest 45-ton breakdown crane on the region, with Bristol and old Oak Common.

'Britannia' No.70028 *Royal Star* easing over the pointwork from the Up Main, across the Relief to the Up Roath Branch (later Up Goods) line at Pengam Jct. with the 12.40 p.m. Cardiff to Manchester train on Sunday, 19th April 1959. The cosmopolitan nature of the train can be seen in this view, with ex-LNER, LMS and Great Western coaches formed into the rake. The Roath branch converged with the Relief again at Rumney Bridge Jct., the rerouting being caused by engineering work on the latter structure to raise it to the full line speed of 75 mph on the mains (and 60 mph on the reliefs), thus removing the previous limit of 60 and 25 mph (respectively) for 'King' class engines between Newport and Cardiff.

Llantrisant pannier No.3663 moving gently along on the Up Relief with target 'Z10', the 4.45 p.m. Llantrisant to Cardiff, on 20th July 1959. The train appears to have been divided at the rear, doubtless for shunting moves into one of the yards. The engine would have soon returned with a load for Llantrisant yard.

'Grange' 4-6-0 No.6852 *Headbourne Grange* (86A) entering Newtown Down Yard under Windsor Road bridge carrying a class 'C' ('4') vacuum freight headcode. This engine was stationed at Bristol St. Philip's Marsh from June 1938 until January 1962, when it was transferred to Newport (Ebbw Jct). Engine headcodes on the Western Region remained as they had been in company days until Monday, 5th June 1950, when a new classification came into being; in this, all goods train headlamp codes with the exception of the old 'J' and 'K' were changed around. In 1960, the letter codes were changed to numerals, though the existing headlamp positions remained.

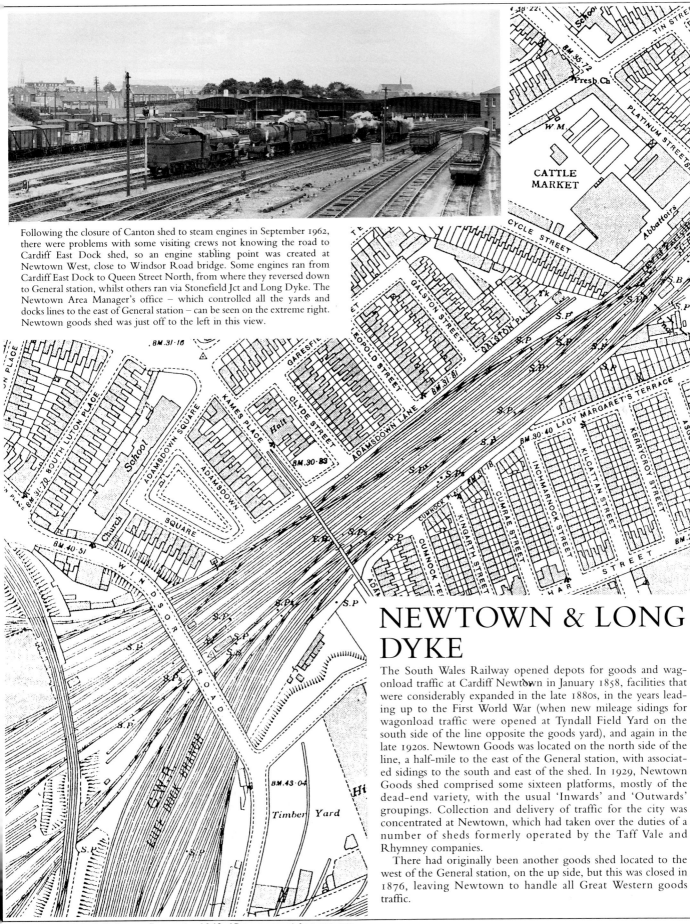

Following the closure of Canton shed to steam engines in September 1962, there were problems with some visiting crews not knowing the road to Cardiff East Dock shed, so an engine stabling point was created at Newtown West, close to Windsor Road bridge. Some engines ran from Cardiff East Dock to Queen Street North, from where they reversed down to General station, whilst others ran via Stonefield Jct and Long Dyke. The Newtown Area Manager's office – which controlled all the yards and docks lines to the east of General station – can be seen on the extreme right. Newtown goods shed was just off to the left in this view.

NEWTOWN & LONG DYKE

The South Wales Railway opened depots for goods and wagonload traffic at Cardiff Newtown in January 1858, facilities that were considerably expanded in the late 1880s, in the years leading up to the First World War (when new mileage sidings for wagonload traffic were opened at Tyndall Field Yard on the south side of the line opposite the goods yard), and again in the late 1920s. Newtown Goods was located on the north side of the line, a half-mile to the east of the General station, with associated sidings to the south and east of the shed. In 1929, Newtown Goods shed comprised some sixteen platforms, mostly of the dead-end variety, with the usual 'Inwards' and 'Outwards' groupings. Collection and delivery of traffic for the city was concentrated at Newtown, which had taken over the duties of a number of sheds formerly operated by the Taff Vale and Rhymney companies.

There had originally been another goods shed located to the west of the General station, on the up side, but this was closed in 1876, leaving Newtown to handle all Great Western goods traffic.

Taken from 25-inch Ordnance Survey for 1942. (Crown copyright reserved)

28

Looking east towards Newtown goods, viewed from the bridge carrying the former Taff Vale East Branch southwards from Queen Street station, with 'Hall' class No.6973 *Bricklehampton Hall* on the Up Relief line below with a coal train. Newtown West box can just be seen under the footbridge, to the left of centre. The line on the extreme left was the headshunt for Newtown Goods, which was located immediately beyond West box.

Long Dyke Yard was located to the east of Newtown shed, on the south side of the running lines, leading into the Bute Dock branch. The yard comprised twelve sidings, mostly through.

A short distance from Newtown, the London & North Western had their own goods depot at Tyndall Street, served from the Rhymney Railway line running from their station at The Parade to the docks.

Following the abandonment of Goods Sundries traffic, the large Newtown Goods complex was closed and recovered by 1976, whilst Long Dyke Yard was taken out of use in 1979, leaving only a group of sidings at Newtown West, these finally being removed in 1983. Tyndall Field Mileage Yard was taken out of use in 1982.

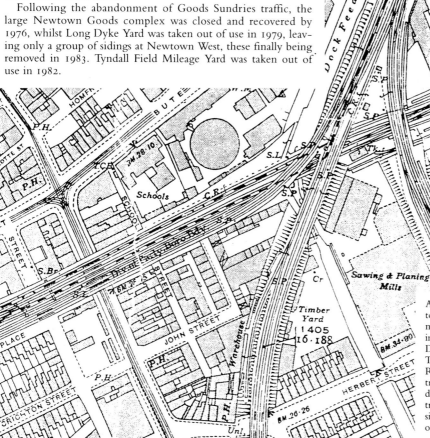

A panoramic view of Newtown Yard, looking west towards General station on 7th August 1965, showing the main goods depot buildings on the right, with the inscription 'BR (W) Express Goods Train Service. One Day Transits between Important Towns' on a gable end. To the left of the shed loop sidings were the Main and Relief lines, with a multiple unit on the Up Main and a train of dead engines en route to the breakers hauled by a diesel on the Down Relief, with No.7923 leading and 6661 trailing. More loops and sidings were located on the south side of the running lines, with Tyndall Field mileage yard on the extreme left.

Taken from 25-inch Ordnance Survey for 1942. (Crown copyright reserved)

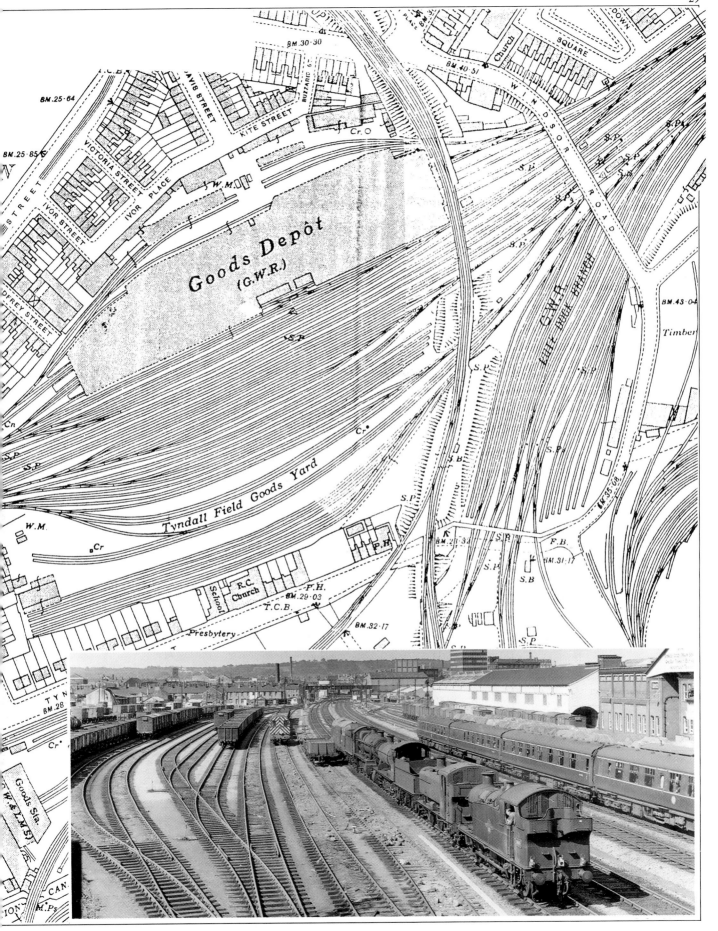

Map labels:

BM.25·64

BM.25·85

BM.30·30

KITE STREET

DAVIS STREET

VICTORIA STREET

IVOR STREET

IVOR PLACE

GODFREY STREET

STREET

Cr. O

J.W.M.

Goods Depôt
(G.W.R.)

S.P.

Cr.

Cn.

S.P.

W.M.

Cr

Tyndall Field Goods Yard

P.H.

R.C.
Church

School

F.H.

BM.29·03

T.C.B.

Presbytery

TY

BM.28

Cr.

Goods Sta.
(W. & L.M.S.)

CAN

ION

M.Ps

BM.40·51

Church

WINDSOR ROAD

SQUARE

DOWN

S.E.

S.P.

S.P.

G.W.R.

LIME DOCK BRANCH

BM.43·04

Timber

S.B.

S.P.

S.P.

BM.36·69

S.P.

S.P.

S.B.

BM.28·32

F.B.

BM.31·17

S.B.

BM.32·17

HOOK STREET

DESPENSER STREET   BM.26.64

DESPENSER GARDENS
BM.26.50

DESPENSER GDNS.

CLARE STREET

BEAUCHAMP STREET

PLANTAGENET STREET

DESPENSER PLACE

Hall

BM.26.56

PO

BM.26.14

FITZHAMON EMBANKMENT

BM.27.43

TRAMWAY

BM.24.34

BM.26.43

T.C.B.

TUDOR STREET

P.H.   L.B.

TRAMWAY

M.25.17

Carriage & Motor Works

TUDOR LANE

BM.21.84

BM.26.61

Printing Works

Wood Street Bridge

BM.31.90

Water Towe

S.L.

S.L.   C.R.

S.L.

S.Ls

S.L.

C.R.

S.L.

S.L.

S.B.

S.R.

S.L.

S.L.

MONMOUTH STREET

Tramway Depôt

BM.25.49

Avana Mills & Bakery

Oilskin Manufactory

Laundry

PENDYRIS STREET

BM.25.52

BM.25.02

Sun. Sch.

Ch.

BM.25.81

BM.24.88

DINAS STREET

HAFOD

TAFFS MEAD

H.W.M.M.T.

MERCHES

BM.25.89

CARDIFF ARMS   Pav.
PARK
1397
16.656

Grand Stand

Football Grou

Grand Stan

RIVER · TAFF

(Afon Taf)

R.E.Hea
(Ter

C.C.L.W.
Ward Bdy.

Duffryn Yard '56XX' class No.6691 struggling up the bank with a heavy train of coal in April 1961, probably destined for SCOW Margam, after having been stopped to cross from the Down Relief to the Down Middle line at Cardiff East to run through General station. The running lines from General station to Queen Street, climbing up on the right, were carried over the main and relief lines by the flyover built in 1896, seen in the middle distance. In the 1950s and 60s, trains using the flyover were through services between Treherbert, Merthyr, Rhymney or Queen Street and Penarth or Barry Island. Just beyond the flyover was another bridge, carrying the line from Bute Road across the main lines, which was mainly used by trains to and from Coryton and Rhymney. The photograph was taken from Cardiff East signal box, an excellent venue for trains approaching from the east.

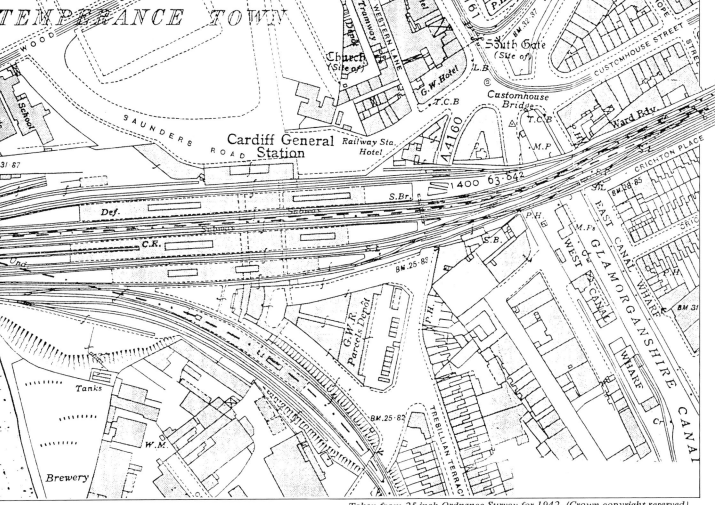

Taken from 25-inch Ordnance Survey for 1942. (Crown copyright reserved)

CARDIFF GENERAL STATION

Opened in 1850 with the Chepstow to Cardiff section of the South Wales Railway, the station was a simple through, two-track design, with sidings to the south and a goods shed to the west. In the latter 1870s, the station was rebuilt to incorporate a four-track section between the platforms, whilst the goods shed was removed. Each platform now had a bay at the departure end.

In 1877, the East Branch Junction, linking the main line with Queen Street station, was authorised. Located about 200 yards east of the General station, the branch was opened in 1881 for mineral traffic and three months later for passenger traffic from and to the Taff Vale Railway. This link was used until 1896 when the present flyover was constructed, at which time the East Branch Jct. was removed.

The Riverside Branch was authorised in 1879, following an agreement with the Marquis of Bute, and opened in 1882 to serve the many industrial concerns along the Glamorganshire Canal and the River Taff, including staithes for coal shipment. In 1893, Barry Railway trains began running through from Cogan into a new platform at Riverside, and a year later both the Barry and Taff Vale Railway commenced through running to a new Cardiff Docks terminus at Clarence Road, at the end of the Riverside Branch.

Cardiff General, east end, with No.6004 *King George III* approaching platform No.3 at the head of the 3.55 p.m. Paddington to Neyland and Fishguard Harbour on Saturday, 26th August 1961. This train was due into Cardiff General at 6.53 p.m., with the sun lowering in the west, and into Fishguard at 10.55 p.m. in time for the 11.45 p.m. boat to Cork (Penrose Quay). In addition to the through vehicles, the 'Capitals United Express' conveyed dining cars as far as Swansea. The 'King' came off at Cardiff, being permitted to run only as far west as Canton shed; authorisation for running of 'Kings' between Newport and Cardiff was granted by 1952, although they did not appear regularly until 1959, after Rumney River Bridge had been altered.

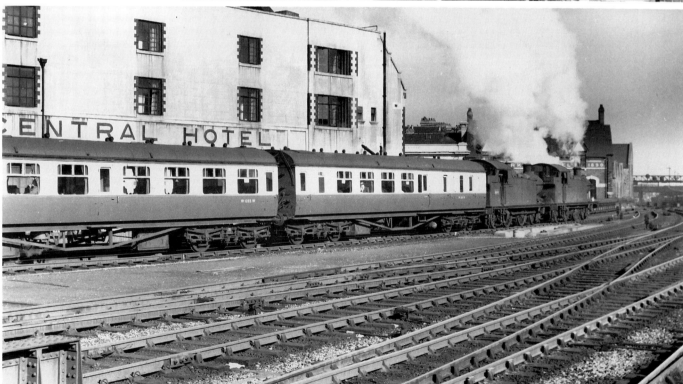

'56XX' class 0-6-2Ts Nos.5630 and 6684 from Radyr departing from No.1 platform on Saturday, 19th October 1957, with a Rhondda Valley to Clifton Down excursion, comprised of ten vestibule coaches. Usually, a 4-6-0 would be rostered for such a duty, but on this occasion the two Valleys engines worked through. The coaches were paper-labelled on the outermost compartment windows; these were often used on relief portions or excursions, where roof destination boards were not appropriate.

Framed by the gantry that spanned the four main tracks at the east end of the station, Canton 'Britannia' No.70026 *Polar Star* is seen entering Cardiff General with the 1.55 p.m. Paddington to Pembroke Dock. This engine would have worked up to London with the 8.0 a.m. Cardiff (6.30 a.m. Swansea – the 'Capitals United'), with a three-hour turnround at Paddington. It still carried handrails on the smoke deflector.

The year 1896 was a landmark in the history of Cardiff as far as the main line route was concerned, with major works at Cardiff General to increase capacity. The sidings to the south of the down bay were removed and the down platform extended to become an island, with an integral westward starting bay. At this time, the up through platform was No.1. the up bay No.2, the north face of the down island No.3, the south face No.4 and the integral bay No.5. An important addition was the creation of another platform (No.6) for use by the Taff Vale Railway trains to and from Queen Street, with a down bay at its west end. Valley trains also now used the new flyover to the east of the station.

New signal boxes were also provided under this work, the East box located where the modern East Box stood, but the West box was placed at the west end of the down platform.

In the early 1920s, a new luggage bridge was provided at the west end of the station, served by electric lifts situated on Nos. 1, 3–5 and 6 platforms. Prior to this, all goods and luggage had to be transferred between platforms by means of the barrow crossing, which had been the source of considerable delays and danger at the busy station.

Another major rebuilding occurred in the early 1930s, affecting not only the General station, but the whole area between Newtown West and Leckwith Jct. As well as new track formations, the section was resignalled with colour lights, replacing the previous semaphores, and with new state-of-the-art signal boxes provided at Cardiff East and Cardiff West (resited), the latter being the largest box in the area, controlling

the vast array of points and signals on the main and local lines as well as the tracks in and out of Canton.

The main up platform was lengthened and made into an island, replacing the previous up bay, and both the up and down main platforms (Nos. 1/2 and 3/4) were made of equal length, with the four-track arrangement between them retained. An integral bay (No.5) remained at the west end of the down island. No.6 platform was made into a full island platform for Valleys trains in place of the previous single face and west end bay, with the new, south-facing through face becoming No.7. The two Riverside platforms, handling the former Barry and Taff Vale Railways services to Barry, Penarth, Cadoxton and Pontypridd (via St. Fagans) trains, were completely remodelled into an island, and associated parcel and holding sidings removed. Additional up loops were provided to increase overall capacity between Leckwith Jct. and Cardiff General, and the Down Relief line extended through to Leckwith Jct.

The station itself was completely rebuilt with a new street-level forecourt and entrance hall provided, twelve feet below rail level, replacing previous structures placed at rail level. Faced externally with Portland stone on a Cornish granite plinth, the inside of the new booking hall was panelled with Devonshire green and Ashburton black marble over the plinth. This new high-roof, single-storey booking hall was a most imposing feature of the rebuilding, with a large glass-fronted booking office on a mahogany base, backing the front wall between the two

Cardiff General station east end, looking west, seen from a departing train c.1959. The Gloucester 'Castle' standing in platform No.1, on the extreme right, was waiting with the 8.48 a.m. Fishguard Harbour to Paddington parcels train, which it would work to Swindon, leaving Cardiff at around 2.30 p.m. An Up Goods line ran to the outside of platform line No.1. The 2.5 p.m. to Bristol alongside platform No.2 was awaiting departure behind two 'Halls'. The two middle roads were normally used by freight traffic and for engine changes, though an occasional non-stop express also utilised them (regularly, the summer 4.25 a.m. Fishguard to Paddington). The two down through platforms (Nos.3 and 4, left of centre) were separated at their western end by a bay (No.5 platform), which was used for parcel vans and an occasional Porthcawl or Swansea service, but during 1965 this was filled in. On the extreme left was another island platform (Nos.6 and 7) serving the ex-Taff Vale/Barry through lines.

entrances. An enquiry office was located at the east end, and the Gower Restaurant at the west end. The entrance and exit points to the subway providing access to the platforms were well separated with the bookstall between, and the usual amenities, such as left luggage office and telephones, were well placed. From the subway, double flights of steps gave access to the main-line platforms (Nos. 1/2 eastwards, 3-5 westwards) with a single flight

to the Valleys platforms (6/7). There was a separate entrance/exit at the Riverside end with its own booking office, again with steps to platforms 8/9 then used for trains to Penarth/Barry and Clarence Road. The parcels office was directly outside the Riverside entrance. The latest type of luggage lifts were provided from each platform, connecting with a subway running from the entrance hall through to the parcels office.

The up 'Red Dragon' (7.30 a.m. Carmarthen) was due out of Cardiff at 10.0 a.m. and into Paddington at 1.0 p.m. after a 145-mile non-stop run via Badminton. On Friday, 30th March 1962, the train was being hauled onwards from General station by Canton 'King' class No.6018 *King Henry V*, which replaced a (scheduled) Landore 'Castle' that had brought the train from Swansea (High Street). A small number of express trains between West Wales and Paddington underwent three engine changes in the course of their journeys, at Carmarthen, Swansea and Cardiff; in the case of the 'Red Dragon', this was the second (and final) engine change.

'42XX' class 2-8-0T No.5217 from Newport (Ebbw Jct) shed approaching Cardiff General on the Up Middle line with an 'H' class train of empty mineral wagons in March 1959. The engine had just been received back after a 'Heavy General' repair at Wolverhampton Stafford Road works. In the late 1950s, 91 of the surviving 150 '42s' were allocated to the Newport Division, eleven of which were at Canton. The train comprised a mixture of steel and wooden mineral wagons.

A portrait of an immaculate Landore 'Castle', No.5016 *Montgomery Castle*, with the up 'Pembroke Coast Express' at No.2 platform on Saturday, 18th March 1961. This train left Pembroke Dock at 1.5 p.m., and was strengthened at Swansea with a portion that included a dining car serving tea and dinner. Due out of Cardiff at 5.0 p.m., the train was scheduled into Paddington at 7.45 p.m. Whilst Canton supplied engines for the earlier departures of the day to London, Landore worked the 5.0, 6.0 and 7.0 p.m. departures, and in some timetables, the 4.0 p.m. too. No.5016 was transferred to Landore from the West of England in May 1938, and remained there until the depot closed in 1961, moving on to Llanelly; she was withdrawn from the latter shed in September 1962. On 1st May 1959, whilst hauling this train, No.5016 was involved in a bad accident near Slough, caused by a broken rail. Seven coaches were derailed, but the engine and the leading two coaches remained on the track, having passed over an eight-inch gap in one of the rails.

After undergoing heavy general repairs at Swindon, Canton's 'Britannias' were normally rostered as the 'top engines' for the 8.0, 10.0 a.m. and 12.0 noon departures for Paddington. Here, No.70015 *Apollo* was returning with the 3.55 p.m. Paddington to Fishguard Harbour, the 'Capitals United Express', watched by admiring porters as she ran into platform No.3. No.70015 was one of three 'Britannias' transferred from Canton to Trafford Park in mid-1958 to work the Manchester & St. Pancras services.

Landore 'Castle' No.5006 *Tregenna Castle* waiting at the colour light signals at the east end of No.2 platform with the 5.20 p.m. Swansea to Paddington express on Sunday, 16th July 1961. Leaving Cardiff at 7.0 p.m., this train was the last up daytime express, calling at Newport, then non-stop to Paddington, where it was due at 10.10 p.m. A dining car was provided from Swansea, in which a leisurely table d'hôte dinner could be enjoyed for 12 shillings. Following her exploits as an Old Oak engine with the 'Cheltenham Flyer' in 1932, when she ran from Swindon to Paddington at an average speed of 71.3 mph, the engine spent several periods at Landore. No.5006 finally moved back to South Wales in March 1958, to Carmarthen, and on to Landore in June 1960, where she remained until that shed closed in September 1961. Perhaps if this famous engine had gone to Woodhams, Barry, on withdrawal in April 1962, she might have been with us today.

Cardiff General, east end, with Old Oak 'Castle' No.5057 *Earl Waldegrave* standing at No.2 platform at the head of the 12.5 p.m. Milford Haven ('A11'), 4.0 p.m. from Cardiff, on Saturday, 29th April 1961. The train number 'A11' was also applied to the 7.45 a.m. Cardiff to Paddington, though with the time differential between the two, no confusion was likely to arise; as Paddington-bound expresses all carried the 'A' series, the attendant numbers 'oo' to '99' were insufficient to cover all trains, and so duplication was necessary. This view was taken from Cardiff East box.

Since their introduction in 1932, the '64XX' engines were employed on auto duties around Cardiff. Here, a Cathays '64' is seen approaching No.7 platform with a service from Coryton and Queen St. to Penarth. Stock comprised trailer No.W225W and an intermediate trailer (compartment Third converted for auto use), possibly W455W or W458W (Dia A41).

From about 1910, the '45XX' class 2-6-2Ts were a common sight in the Newport area and around Tondu, and from the early 1930s, in West Wales, too. It was not until the introduction of the Valleys regular interval service in September 1953 that several of the '4575' variant were converted for auto working and allocated to Cathays and Barry. Their use on anything other than auto trains (including double-autos) was uncommon, but one day in the summer of 1961, Cathays used No.5568 to work a 6-coach special ('X09'), probably to Barry Island; it is seen here passing Cardiff East Box on its way into platform No.7. The leading two vehicles were 9ft 3in-wide stock, with recessed door and commode handles; these were quite common on Valleys trains. The rear of the train was a four-set.

It was very unusual to find a regular Valleys train double-headed, but on this occasion Treherbert was required to send a '56XX' locomotive to work a special back from Barry Island, and it was positioned inside the train engine. This view shows the Treherbert passenger turn 'TC', 4.30 p.m. Treherbert to Barry Island, approaching No.7 platform behind Standard 'Class 3MT' 2-6-2T No.82032 and No.5613. This diagram covered four round trips between Treherbert and Barry Island, routed via Pontypridd, Cardiff Queen Street and General stations, and Cogan, with the usual summer season six-coach train.

It was not often that two main-line trains arrived simultaneously at General station from the same direction, though on summer Saturdays, a down terminating express might be diverted into platform No.7 when 3 and 4 were already occupied. In this case, the 9.15 a.m. Blackpool North to Cardiff (Train No.300, Saturdays only) had topped the climb and was easing its train off the Down Relief, on which it had travelled from Newtown, to enter No.7 platform behind Canton Standard 'Class 5' 4-6-0 No.73024 on 31st August 1957. Following the Blackpool train can be seen No.4964 *Rodwell Hall* (Canton) on the 10.10 a.m. Paignton (Train 585), approaching on the Down Main, destined for platform No.4; this service was due into Cardiff at 2.50 p.m., twenty-five minutes before the Blackpool.

If capacity permitted, freight trains for the Barry line would be brought along the Down Relief line from Newtown West and routed to run across through platform No.7 at General station, rather than through the Down Middle road and crossed for Barry at Cardiff West or Penarth Curve South. This picture shows Barry's resplendent '56XX' No.5619 approaching Cardiff General with the mineral 'B31' duty – a service booked to run from Cadoxton to Peterston and Aber Jct. However, it is seen here making its way home on this occasion with a train of empty banana vans bound for Geest at Barry Docks. A very heavy flow of banana traffic normally ran from Sunday evening until mid-week, and required the prompt return of vans in readiness for the next load.

The 3.15 p.m. Barry Docks to Acton banana train standing on the Up Middle behind 'Castle' No.5014 *Goodrich Castle* from Old Oak shed. Geest banana traffic commenced from Barry Docks in the late 1950s, supplementing similar traffic from Avonmouth and Southampton. As Paddington insisted that banana trains be dealt with as 'special traffic', for which no diagrammed main line power was provided, the engines were arranged through the Control. Unbalanced Old Oak engines were often worked home on such traffic. The down train of mineral wagons approaching would probably have used the Down Middle road to pass through the station.

'Hall' No.4958 *Priory Hall* of Carmarthen shed arriving at No.2 platform with an up football special (No.06) from Llanelly on Saturday, 18th October 1958. The first vehicle in the ten-coach train was a Van Third of the 1935 'Centenary' stock, with other pre-nationalisation coaches forming the rest of the train.

Very little passenger traffic passed non-stop through Cardiff General station. One notable exception was the 4.25 a.m. Fishguard to Paddington (Train No.712), seen here running through on the Up Middle road behind Old Oak 'Castle' No.5084 *Reading Abbey* on Saturday, 30th July 1955.

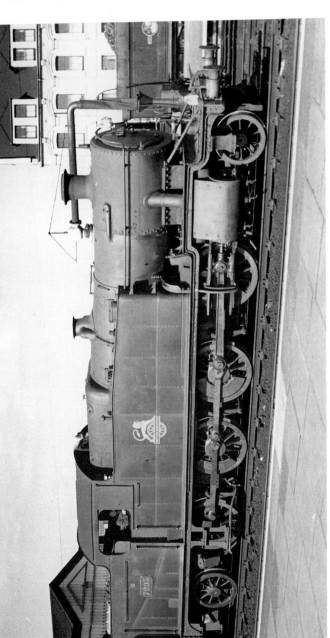

'Britannia' No.70024 *Vulcan* backing down onto 'The Red Dragon' at No.2 platform in April 1961. With a 10.0 a.m. departure from Cardiff, the train called at Newport, then ran non-stop to Paddington for a 1.0 p.m. arrival. The engine and crew returned from Paddington to Cardiff with the 3.55 p.m. 'Capitals United Express', due in at 6.53 p.m. giving a 9½-hour turn off shed for the crew, though the engine continued through to Swansea. No.70024 had a long spell of London workings during that year, following a Heavy General repair at Swindon.

Llanelly '72XX' class 2-8-2T No.7203 on the middle road at Cardiff General with an up class 'H' mineral train from Margam c.1958. The east end of platform No.3 was an excellent venue for such portraits of standing engines. No.7203 was built from '42XX' class 2-8-0T No.5278 in September 1934 as part of a batch of 20, and retained that engine's raised footplating over the cylinders, with curved drop ends.

Apart from a couple of Swindon-based examples which sometimes appeared on freight services, the 'Earl' (later 90XX) class 4-4-0s were not a familiar sight at Cardiff. No.9017 was utilised on 12th May 1956 for part of a Gloucestershire Railway Society special into the Valleys, which also involved '2301' class 0-6-0 No.2538 and ex-Taff Vale Class 'A' 0-6-2T No.391. Here, the 'Earl' was standing on the Up Goods line alongside platform No.1 awaiting the return of the special, which it worked forward from Cardiff to Gloucester. In the latter 1950s, the survivors of the class were to be found at Croes Newydd or at ex-Cambrian sheds; 9017 was a Machynlleth engine. This engine now resides on the Bluebell Railway as No.3217 *Earl of Berkeley*.

In January 1957, Canton received the full allocation of Western Region 'Britannias', with Nos.70015-24 joining the five (70025-29) already stationed there. The concentration of the class at Canton gave better utilisation and availability, and the engines were accepted by the Canton men, who were performing very well with their original five engines. The 'Britannias' had not been particularly popular with crews at their previous sheds – Old Oak (five engines), Newton Abbot (one) and Laira (four). Although three were transferred away to Trafford Park in 1958, the remainder stayed at Canton until 1961, during which time they dominated the principal express services from that shed. Engines were changed at Cardiff on several London-bound expresses. Here, No.70028 *Royal Star* had brought the 8.0 a.m. Neyland (Train A58) into Cardiff in summer 1960, was to be replaced by No.70025 *Western Star* for the run to Paddington.

A fine portrait of No.70027 *Rising Star* on the Up Middle road, awaiting the arrival of its train (the 8.0 a.m. Neyland) for a 12 noon departure to Paddington on 11th May 1957. The sight of a gleaming 'Britannia' gliding up the Middle road light from Canton would never fail to attract the attention of waiting passengers, staff or enthusiasts.

Bristol passenger engines were a common sight at Cardiff, either working in trains from Temple Meads, or from the Southern Region via Salisbury. The prototype 4-6-0 'County', No.1000 *County of Middlesex*, from Bath Road shed, is seen here alongside No.4 platform with the 4.25 p.m. Cardiff to Portsmouth train, and also worked the 11.0 a.m. Brighton to Cardiff and the 6.40 p.m. Swansea (from Cardiff) to Bristol the following day as part of a three-day cycle involving mostly Southern Region through trains. This turn had remained largely intact since the early 1950s, and possibly earlier.

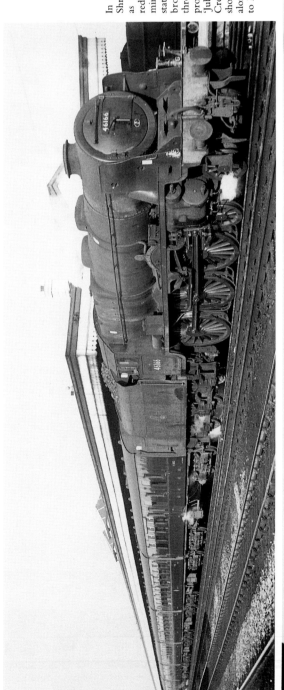

In March 1962, work on Castle Foregate bridge, Shrewsbury, dictated that as little engine changing as possible should take place at Shrewsbury, to reduce the level of occupation over the bridge by minimising the light engine movements between station and shed. Thus, the LMR locomotives that brought the trains into Shrewsbury worked through, in some instances to Cardiff, and this provided a fascinating selection of 'Royal Scots', 'Jubilees' and rebuilt 'Patriots' from Longsight, Crewe North and even Polmadie sheds. This view shows 'Royal Scot' No. 46166 *London Rifle Brigade* alongside No.2 platform with the 8.55 a.m. Cardiff to Manchester on Friday, 16th March 1962.

By lunchtime on summer Saturdays, sheds were often scraping the bottom of the barrel for motive power. So it was on Saturday, 22nd August 1959, when all Canton could find for the 1.15 p.m. Cardiff to Birmingham (train 880) was LMR '8F' 2-8-0 No.48347, which is seen here at No.2 platform. With the fairly leisurely Saturday timings on these services, the '8F' would probably have acquitted itself quite well.

A more usual duty for an '8F' was a through goods, and Llanelly's No.48328 is seen here on a down class 'E' express freight on the Down Middle road at Cardiff General on Wednesday, 15th March 1961. Llanelly had a number of these engines, mainly for work on the Central Wales line, but they would occasionally appear on main-line work.

Standing in all her polished glory with the 10.0 a.m. up 'Red Dragon', this view shows Canton's 'Castle' No.5099 *Compton Castle* waiting at No.2 platform for the 'right away' on Saturday, 6th February 1960. This engine was rated by the Canton shedmaster as one of the best ever 'Castles', and would have experienced little difficulty with the timing of this train. That this was in the period of 'Britannia' dominance speaks volumes for the quality of this engine.

In September 1960, six 'Kings' were allocated to Canton for workings to Paddington and Shrewsbury. Here No.6023 *King Edward II* was waiting in the Up Middle road at General station to take over up 'Red Dragon', the 10.0 a.m. Cardiff (7.30 Carmarthen) to Paddington on Saturday, 22nd April 1961. As usual, the engine was scheduled to work back with the 3.55 p.m. Paddington. 'Kings' were restricted to Cardiff General and Canton shed, and could not therefore work onwards to Swansea, as could the 'Britannias' and 'Castles'. The shed code plate 88A (Canton, from January 1961), later signified Cardiff East Dock, which took over as the main line steam shed from Canton in September 1962.

'9F' class 2-10-0 No.92152 from Saltley (Birmingham) at No.4 platform on Monday, 28th August 1961, with a 'C' class pigeon special, comprising a Brake Third for the handlers and a string of vans for their feathered charges. The pigeon special was a very common sight in the interwar period, but less so by this time. Prior to the general through working of LMR engines to Cardiff from about 1962, it was rare for such a working to take place. Engines of through workings would usually be changed at Gloucester, due to engine restrictions that would not permit the through working of LMR locomotives beyond Over Junction on the South Wales line.

Rhymney's '51XX' class 2-6-2T No.4152 with the 9.35 a.m. Penarth to Rhymney passenger (turn 'RF') at No.6 platform on Friday, 30th August 1957. The '51s' appeared on Valley duties as early as 1942, working from Cathays and Ferndale, and soon afterwards from Treherbert and Rhymney. By the latter 1950s, Rhymney was a sub-shed of Merthyr (88D), though these ex-GWR outside-cylinder engines were prevented from working to Merthyr because of insufficient clearances. Standard 'Class 3s' gradually took over the whole of the Rhondda and Merthyr line trains from September 1953, although the Rhymney line remained in the hands of '41XXs' and '56XXs'. The vehicle on the right was a Dia.022 inside-frame 'Siphon G'.

Riverside station was opened in 1893, and was used by the Taff Vale company for their services to Penarth and Cadoxton, and by the Barry Railway for their trains to Barry (Barry Island from 1896), the Vale of Glamorgan (from 1897) and Pontypridd (via St. Fagans). From 1894, trains began running through to and from the new station at Clarence Road. This view shows Radyr 2-6-2T No.4164 pulling away from Riverside down platform (No.9) with the 3.48 p.m. to Penarth and Cadoxton on Friday, 10th October 1958.

Abercynon turn 'JB' ran all day around the Cardiff area, working services to Pontypridd via St. Fagans, and from Queen Street or Riverside to Penarth. '64XX' class engines Nos.6411 and 6438 were regularly employed; No.6438 is seen here at No.7 platform at General station with a morning service from Queen Street to Penarth on Saturday, 12th October 1957. The train comprised a compartment trailer and an auto coach.

The basic regular interval service introduced in September 1953 between Treherbert or Merthyr and Barry Island was worked by Standard 'Class 3' 2-6-2Ts that normally ran two round trips per turn. Barry depot provided two engines each day for Merthyr services as their part of the workings. Here, No.84042 is seen at platform No.7 with the 2.0 p.m. Merthyr to Barry Island (Merthyr 'MC' turn) on Thursday, 6th March 1958; it would return from Barry to Merthyr with a late afternoon peak hour train. The first vehicle, a former LMR Brake Second, was released when the Merthyr, Tredegar & Abergavenny passenger service closed, and used by Merthyr in a Barry set.

Radyr only received 'Class 3' 2-6-2Ts after Barry and Treherbert had lost their examples with dieselisation. This picture shows Radyr's No.82034 at Riverside on Wednesday, 2nd April 1958, with the 4.20 p.m. to Penarth and Cadoxton. The passenger duty 'CJ' was a Cathays turn before the transfer of all Cathays duties to Radyr, when the former depot was converted for DMU operations. Originally, Riverside station comprised two separate platforms, but was converted into a 600ft-long single-island arrangement in the rebuilding of the site in the early 1930s.

'51XX' class No.4163 taking water at Riverside prior to working the 3.48 p.m. to Cadoxton ('CC' duty) via Penarth in 1958. This engine had originally been allocated to both Barry and Rhymney, but was, by this time, at Radyr. The Cadoxton services were a continuation of the former Taff Vale services to Penarth and Cadoxton (originally Biglis Jct.). There was much acrimony between the Taff and Barry companies over this service, and the latter initially took pleasure in refusing Taff Vale trains access to the terminus, probably on the grounds of heavy line occupation by its own coal shipment traffic.

Those 'Britannias' and 'Castles' at Canton that had accumulated high mileages since their last general repair at Swindon were mostly utilised on trains to the west of Cardiff, or on 'C' class traffic to Swindon. Here No.70025 *Western Star* was entering No.2 platform at Cardiff General station with the 8.0 a.m. Neyland to Paddington, which it took over at Swansea (10.30 a.m. departure). At Cardiff, it would hand the train over to a low-mileage 'Britannia' for a 12.0 noon departure to Paddington. In the winter timetable during the late 1950s, this train was formed of coaches from Swansea (4, including dining car), Neyland (3). Fishguard Harbour (2) and Pembroke Dock (3). During the summer months at that time, the train was divided, with a section from Pembroke Dock running thirty minutes ahead of the main train to Paddington.

Treherbert '82XXX' class 2-6-2T No.82032 entering No.6 platform with the 3.50 p.m. Barry Island to Treherbert (target 'TD'), a journey of 32 miles that took around 1 hour 40 minutes. Here the standard five-coach set was strengthened at the front by an ex-GWR Dia.E96 9-compartment 'Toplight' non-corridor Composite.

The '31XXs' of 1938 were a class of just five locomotives, numbered 3100-04, rebuilds of earlier '3150' class engines with 5ft 3in wheels in place of the former 5ft 8in. The intention was to rebuild all 41, although the Second World War put a stop to further work. Of these, four engines were withdrawn between May 1957 and October 1958, leaving No.3103 in traffic until January 1960; this engine is seen here at No.4 platform with a Newport to Ninian Park football excursion on 15th March 1958, formed of a 6-coach articulated set which was used in the area for a while, and a couple of additional vehicles at the rear.

The last 'Star' in traffic, No.4056 *Princess Margaret*, worked regularly between Bristol and Cardiff in the latter 1950s, and is pictured here at No.4 platform at the head of a down express on Saturday, 13th July 1957. She was dispatched from her home depot, Bath Road, to Swindon in September 1957, and withdrawn from service the following month. The first vehicle was a 'Sunshine' Van Third.

The 8.20 am. Hereford to Cardiff Parcels worked empty vans into Cardiff, and ran through to Canton without being platformed. It was worked between Hereford and Pontypool Road by a Hereford 'Hall' and onwards by '56XX' class 0-6-2Ts, alternating from Pontypool Road and Canton sheds. Here No.6644 was running through the Down Middle road en route to Canton Carriage Sidings on Thursday, 26th September 1957. The train included a BR fish van, ex-LNER vehicles and a 'Siphon G'.

No.4278 passing through Cardiff General on the Up Middle road with an 'H' class mixed through freight on 3rd March 1958, probably bound for Newport or Severn Tunnel Jct. The varied selection of flat, open (one sheeted) and covered (box) goods wagons, recall the age of the unfitted goods train that was soon to pass into history. Although outside steampipes were fitted to some of the earlier batches of the class from the 1930s, No.4278 did not receive the modification.

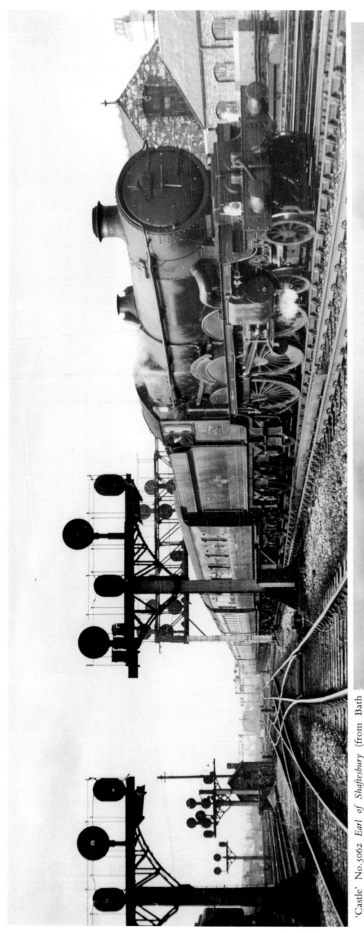

'Castle' No.5062 *Earl of Shaftesbury* (from Bath Road shed) moving off the Up Main onto the No.2 platform road at the west end of General station. The train was an afternoon relief to Paddington, October 1958. The colour lights dated from the 1934 signalling scheme.

Landore 'Castle' No.5091 *Cleeve Abbey* leaving Cardiff General on the Down Main with train No.714, the 8.55 a.m. Paddington to Pembroke Dock in June 1959. After the 1958 summer service, the train numbering system had been altered; the '7XX' series previously identified up South Wales services, and '714' had been the 3.55 a.m. Fishguard train. The photograph was taken from the extensive junctions in front of Cardiff West box, under the watchful eye of the signalman. With ten 'Castles' diagrammed to work to Paddington at this time, Landore required a good supply of serviceable engines. The shed maintained them in an immaculate condition, and they were immediately recognisable by the silver-painted buffers.

On the approach to No.2 platform, 'Grange' No.6802 *Bampton Grange* (Pontypool Road) with a Collett flush-bottom 3,500-gallon tender (Lot 118) assisting 'Hall' No. 6928 *Underley Hall* (Shrewsbury) with the empty stock forming the 4.40 p.m. Cardiff to Manchester (London Road) on Saturday, 29th August 1959. Double-heading often occurred on this service: train No.717 was the 9.15 a.m. Manchester to Swansea, which the 'Grange' had previously worked down from Pontypool Road, whilst the 'Hall' had earlier brought in the 9.5 a.m. Birkenhead, working southwards from Shrewsbury. The numbering pamphlet for 1959 gives train No.960 for the 4.40 p.m. Cardiff, which would be carried between Cardiff and Shrewsbury.

Penarth East Curve swung around through about 120 degrees between Penarth Curve South and Cardiff West boxes, and was subject to a permanent 25 mph speed limit. This view shows Radyr '51XX' class No.4129 negotiating the curve with an evening train from Penarth to Queen Street on Thursday, 12th June 1958. The sidings on the extreme right of the picture holding passenger stock were originally installed by the Barry Railway to hold coal traffic bound for Barry Docks.

The 8.55 a.m. Paddington to Pembroke Dock departing from Cardiff General station behind Landore 'Castle' No.7018 *Drysllwyn Castle* on Saturday, 16th July 1955. The train also conveyed through vehicles for Neyland, with a Hawksworth Van Third, a 70ft 'Toplight' and a rebuilt 70ft Dining Car destined for Swansea at the head. A month after this photograph was taken, No.7018 was to undergo extensive trials on the Swindon Test Plant, after which she was fitted with a double chimney. She was then transferred to Bath Road shed to work the 'Bristolian'. The photograph was taken from Clare Road bridge, from which there was a pathway leading to West box.

Seen from alongside the Down Relief line, 'Castle' No.5011 *Tintagel Castle* passing Cardiff West Jct. with the 7.55 a.m. Paddington to Swansea (Train 'F11') on Wednesday, 15th March 1961. This train was one of the shortest long-distance expresses to leave Paddington, with just six coaches, formed Brake Compo, Dining Car, First, two Seconds and a Van Second, all bound for Swansea. The engine carried Old Oak's '81A' shedplate, and was working OOC turn No.18, which involved the 7.55 a.m. as far as Swansea, returning with the 9.35 p.m. Swansea (6.50 p.m. Neyland) to Paddington.

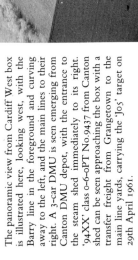

Another view from Clare Road bridge, showing 'Hall' No.5913 *Rushton Hall* (from Landore shed) approaching No.2 platform with the coaches for the 11.40 a.m. Cardiff to Gloucester service on 30th August 1958. The engine had brought the coaches from Canton carriage shed, the lines from which approached West box sandwiched between the main running lines to Swansea and the Penarth lines. The stock comprised a Hawksworth Passenger Brake Van, with a four-coach corridor train set.

The panoramic view from Cardiff West box is illustrated here, looking west, with the Barry line in the foreground and curving away to the left, and the main lines to their right. A 3-car DMU is seen emerging from Canton DMU depot, with the entrance to the steam shed immediately to its right. '94XX' class 0-6-0PT No.9437 from Canton shed can be seen approaching the box with a transfer freight from Grangetown to the main line yards, carrying the 'J05' target on 29th April 1961.

As with Canton express engines, the ex-works Landore 'Castles' would immediately be rostered on the top turns to Paddington. No.7016 *Chester Castle* had emerged from Swindon in October 1958 from a Heavy General repair, and is seen in that month with the down 8.50 a.m. Paddington to Swansea 'South Wales Pullman' as it approached Canton. The train returned at 4.35 p.m. from Swansea, but was not a commercial success; however, when the running was reversed in 1961 with the introduction of the diesel 'Blue Pullman', which left Swansea at 6.40 a.m. and Paddington at 4.55 p.m., the trains were often fully booked well in advance with business travellers. First class Pullman cars carried a name, Second class numbers.

'56XX' No.6691 from Duffryn Yard shed approaching Canton on the Down Relief road with a train of empty mineral wagons bound for collieries in West Glamorgan on Monday, 27th November 1961. In the opposite direction, a '43XX' can be seen approaching with a loaded train. The distinctive footbridge connected De Croche Place (to the right) with the carriage shed, passing over the engine shed roads on the way.

The 2.30 p.m. Neyland to Paddington (7.0 p.m. Cardiff) passing Canton behind Landore 'Castle' No.7012 'Barry Castle' on Monday, 25th June 1956, overtaking Canton 'Austerity' No.90148 with a freight on the Up Relief. Canton 'Castle' No.5007 Rougemont Castle, standing on one of the shed sidings alongside the former coal stage, was awaiting the arrival of the 12.45 p.m. Old Oak to Neyland/Whitland fish and milk empties, which it would work forward. The long building on the left was formerly the carriage shed, but during the 1930s development was converted into a milk depot. It also handled parcels traffic, particularly Zetters football pools mail in the 'sixties.

The 12.45 p.m. Old Oak to Neyland fish empties (and milk empties for Whitland) standing on the Down Relief behind Gloucester '43XX' No.4358. An engine change was about to take place, and the fireman of the '43' had just lifted the lamp from over the left-hand buffer ('C' class train), leaving the light engine code ('G') showing. No.5007 would ease forward after 4358 had moved off its train. On the Up Relief, 'Castle' No.5009 Shrewsbury Castle (Swindon shed) can be seen moving off with the 3.50 p.m. Whitland to Kensington milk, which had just been remanned by Canton men, who worked the train to Swindon. The engine took over the milk train at Felin Fran, another location used for engine changes.

Having taken over the fish and milk empties, No.5007 *Rougemont Castle* was waiting for departure at 7.6 p.m.; the engine returned the next day on the 3.50 p.m. Milford Haven to Paddington fish as far as Canton. At this time of day, the 10.35 a.m. Kensington to Whitland milk empties and the 12.45 p.m. Old Oak to Neyland fish empties called at Canton, one after the other. The milk empties was denoted 'run as required', and it seems logical that, loads permitting, the two trains would be combined to save engine power and line occupation. The old coaling stage with the water tower above, on the east side of Canton shed, can be seen to the right; a new, larger structure was provided on the south side of the shed in the early 1930s, giving a much-increased capacity. Penarth East curve may be seen in the distance beyond the building.

Two Swindon 'Castles' – Nos.5000 *Launceston Castle* and 5023 *Brecon Castle* – heading the 3.50 p.m. Whitland to Kensington milk away from Canton after the stop for remanning on Tuesday, 28th April 1959. The train engine had worked down with the 1.0 a.m. Paddington to Swansea, and had spent the day on Landore shed.

'Hall' No.6905 *Claughton Hall* from Landore, marshalling vehicles at the milk depot while working the 7.10 p.m. Cardiff to Swansea parcels, c. 1958. In addition to parcels vehicles, this train worked churn traffic from Cardiff to Carmarthen, the vehicles having worked up the previous evening on the 7.50 p.m. Neyland parcels (due Cardiff 2.45 a.m.). The tender was No.2586, the 8-wheeled vehicle it ran with from around 1958. No.6905 worked up to Cardiff with the 8.30 a.m. Swansea ('The Red Dragon') that morning, and was returning with the headboard reversed.

A down Sunday afternoon troop train passing Canton behind No.5326 of St. Philip's Marsh shed. Such duties were usually worked by 'Halls' or 'Granges' and, with eleven coaches in the train, a 4-6-0 would probably have been more appropriate power. Nevertheless, with the fireman taking it easy, the '43' obviously had the task well in hand.

'Castle' No.5085 *Evesham Abbey* with the 2.55 p.m. Paddington to Swansea (Train 'F47') on Monday, 22nd May 1961. The engine was allocated to Bristol St. Philip's Marsh, not a usual source of power for London to South Wales trains, and was probably deputizing for a Landore engine. The 10.35 a.m. Kensington to Whitland and Neyland milk empties on the Down Relief had changed engines to Canton 'Britannia' No.70025 *Western Star*, which was due to return with the 3.50 p.m. Milford Haven fish.

Landore 'Castle' No.5013 *Abergavenny Castle* accelerating away through Canton with the 8.55 a.m. Paddington to Pembroke Dock (714) in September 1960. The usual up working for this duty was the 4.30 p.m. Swansea to Paddington ('The South Wales Pullman') the previous day. '42XX' class 2-8-0T No.4213 from Duffryn Yard can be seen on the Up Relief with a freight train.

'43XX' 2-6-0 No.5398 from Gloucester shed standing on the Down Goods at Canton with the 10.35 a.m. Kensington milk empties train for Whitland c.1958. The engine was due to return to Swindon with the 5.15 p.m. Whitland to Paddington milk train, leaving Canton at 8.45 p.m., some three hours after this photograph was taken; it was unlikely that Canton would have allowed a 'Mogul' on such a duty.

Old Oak 'Castle' No.7020 *Gloucester Castle* with an up express passing under the footbridge at Canton on Sunday, 16th February 1958. Train No.178 was the 6.55 p.m. Paddington to Fishguard in the winter 1957/8 timetable, and the engine was probably working the return of the Saturday trip, the 11.20 a.m. (Sundays) Carmarthen to Paddington (12.20 p.m. Swansea), though with the down train number still displayed.

'56XX' class No.5683 passing Canton with a diverted service from Rhymney to Cardiff on Sunday, 25th February 1962. These trains usually ran in from the north via Caerphilly and Queen Street, but on this occasion, due to engineering work, the service approached the station from the west, having been rerouted via Penrhos Jct. and onto the former Barry route to Tynycaeau Jct. and St. Fagans, where it joined the main line. The load was only 4 coaches, in place of the usual standard 5-coach set.

A mixed 'H' class freight behind 2-8-0T No.4213, ex-Caerphilly works after a Heavy Intermediate repair, passing Canton box in September 1960. The engine was from Duffryn Yard shed, and the train probably originated from the Swansea or Margam area. Behind the freight, this view also shows numerous horseboxes in Canton yard, with a long string of opens on the mileage siding. The London Brick Company also used this yard regularly in the 1950s, and coal was another common traffic here.

Landore 'Castle' No.7028 *Cadbury Castle* passing Canton box with the 8.0 a.m. Neyland to Paddington service on Friday, 14th February 1958. The engine was working the train as far as Cardiff General station, where it was taken forward at noon by a Canton 'Britannia'. At the start of the 1957/8 timetable, this duty was part of a two-day cycle which took the 'Castle' on with the 3.20 p.m. to Bristol, thence with the 12.0 noon Penzance to Pontypool Road, and from there back to Cardiff with through coaches from Manchester, off the 8.20 p.m. Crewe. The following day, the engine worked to Gloucester and back before returning to Swansea with an evening train. As dieselisation gradually spread into the cross-country turns, steam duties such as these altered radically. No.7028 went to Landore when new in June 1950, moving on to Llanelly when the Swansea shed closed in 1960 for conversion into a diesel depot.

'43XX' class 2-6-0s Nos.5336 and 6345 on the Up Relief lines waiting at Canton box for a road through Cardiff station in October 1959. No.5336 (Severn Tunnel Jct.) was on a 'D' class express freight, and would probably have priority over 6345 (Llanelly) and her train, which carried 'H' class lamps. Well over a hundred '43s' were still in traffic in 1962, and some 35 survived into 1964.

The 'C' class 3.35 p.m. Fishguard Harbour to Paddington vacuum freight is seen behind 'Hall' class No.5908 *Moreton Hall* (from Goodwick shed) at Canton box in the evening of Monday, 9th July 1956. The engine was about to be changed for the 'Hall' seen in the distance, making its way alongside the shed. This train could be quite heavy, but is lighter on this occasion for the want of the usual cattle traffic.

Severn Tunnel Jct. '28XX' class No.2854 pausing near Canton box with an up class 'H' coal train c. 1960. By this time, few wooden coal wagons were to be seen in such trains, and steel mineral types dominated. However, there were still a number of wooden wagons in use for other purposes in the mileage yard behind.

'Castle' No.5051 *Earl Bathurst* clearing Canton with the down 'South Wales Pullman', 8.50 a.m. Paddington to Swansea, on Thursday, 31st August 1961. The stock returned as the 4.30 p.m. Swansea that afternoon. '56XX' No.5612, with '42XX' No.4298 dead inside (both engines from Llanelly), can be seen beyond on the Up Relief with a goods train containing steelwork, possibly from the Swansea area. No.4298 had a rough year: she had been stopped twice earlier in the year at Ebbw Jct. for casual repair, and had been out of service at Llanelly shed since June; the engine was now being hauled dead for a Heavy Casual repair to Caerphilly works, which she entered on 27th September.

CANTON ENGINE SHED

The first main-line engine shed was located at Long Dyke, just east of Newtown Yard, and was closed in 1882 when the depot was transferred to Canton. At Canton, the new shed was built as a six-road straight shed with a turntable (roundhouse) shed at the west end, and a coal stage (with water tank over) and a turntable at the east end of the shed site. As part of the 1896 expansion of facilities, Canton shed was considerably enlarged, with 55ft turntables and an extension to the coaling stage. In 1899 a new carriage shed was opened on the up side, opposite the engine shed (the later milk depot).

The improvement of facilities between 1931-4 saw a new coaling plant on the south side of the shed site, and a new 65ft turntable at the west end of the shed, replacing the turntable and installations at the east end, though the old coaling plant (and water tower) remained in situ until the closure of the depot in 1962. A 55ft turntable remained in the roundhouse. The main development of 1934 was, however, the construction of a new 11-track carriage shed south of the engine shed, at which time the former carriage shed on the up side became a milk and parcels depot. With the coming of the diesel era, Canton engine shed was closed in September 1962 for conversion to a Diesel Servicing and Maintenance Depot, and, by this time, DMU servicing facilities had also been built into the carriage shed.

On the motive power side, Cardiff Canton was always one of the top express passenger depots on the Great Western. At the turn of the century, Canton had an allocation of around 80 engines, goods locomotives comprising 0-6-0s of the 'Standard' and '2301' classes, and 0-6-0 tanks of the '1016', '1076', '1854' and '2721' designs. Passenger engines were mostly 2-4-0s of the '806' and '2201'

design, with a few 'Stella', 'Achilles' 4-2-2s, and '3232' locomotives. '3521' and 'Bulldog' 4-4-0s completed the main allocation.

Following the opening of Fishguard Harbour in 1906 and the handling of Transatlantic liners there from 1909-13, the depot received a fleet of the latest 'Saint' and 'Star' class 4-6-0s from 1907 onwards. For heavy freight work, the first '28XX' arrived at Canton in 1912.

The first 'Castle' arrived in 1929. In that year, the shed was very much a mixture of the old and new, with 4-6-0 'Saints', 'Stars' and 'Halls', '30XX' 2-8-0s, '26XX' and '43XX' 2-6-0s, '2301' class 0-6-0s, 'Bulldog' and 'Armstrong' 4-4-0s and numerous examples of older classes of 0-6-0 tanks with a few examples of the newer '56XX' and '57XXs'. The total allocation was now around 105 locomotives. In the years following, the more modern classes expanded in numbers at the expense of the old, and '68XX' 4-6-0s, '72XX' 2-8-2Ts and '64XX' (auto) 0-6-0PTs all made their appearances. Even so, the '2301' 0-6-0s and old 0-6-0 tanks were still a very familiar sight around the shed. Following the closure of the Taff Vale depot at Penarth Dock in 1929, Canton took much of its allocation of Taff, Barry and Rhymney Railway absorbed 0-6-2T engines to cover work previously undertaken by that depot.

In the war years, 'USA', 'WD Austerity' and LMS '8F' 2-8-0s variously were all shedded at Canton, whilst the '28XXs' expanded in numbers considerably.

Due to the restrictions placed on 'King' class engines, they were only authorised to Cardiff in 1952, with full running powers from 1959. Thus, from the late 1920s until after nationalisation, Canton relied on its fleet of 'Castles' for all its top link work to London and Shrewsbury.

A pair of 'Britannias' parked underneath the distinctive footbridge at the east end of Canton shed in summer 1960. No.70022 *Tornado* was scheduled to work the 1.13 p.m. from Cardiff to Shrewsbury (11.50 a.m. Swansea to Manchester Piccadilly) and the 5.6 p.m. return, a Plymouth-bound train that conveyed the 2.50 p.m. through coaches from Liverpool Lime St. to Cardiff. No.70020 *Mercury* standing alongside with 'A58' boards was for the 12.0 noon Cardiff to Paddington (8.0 a.m. Neyland), with the 5.55 p.m. return.

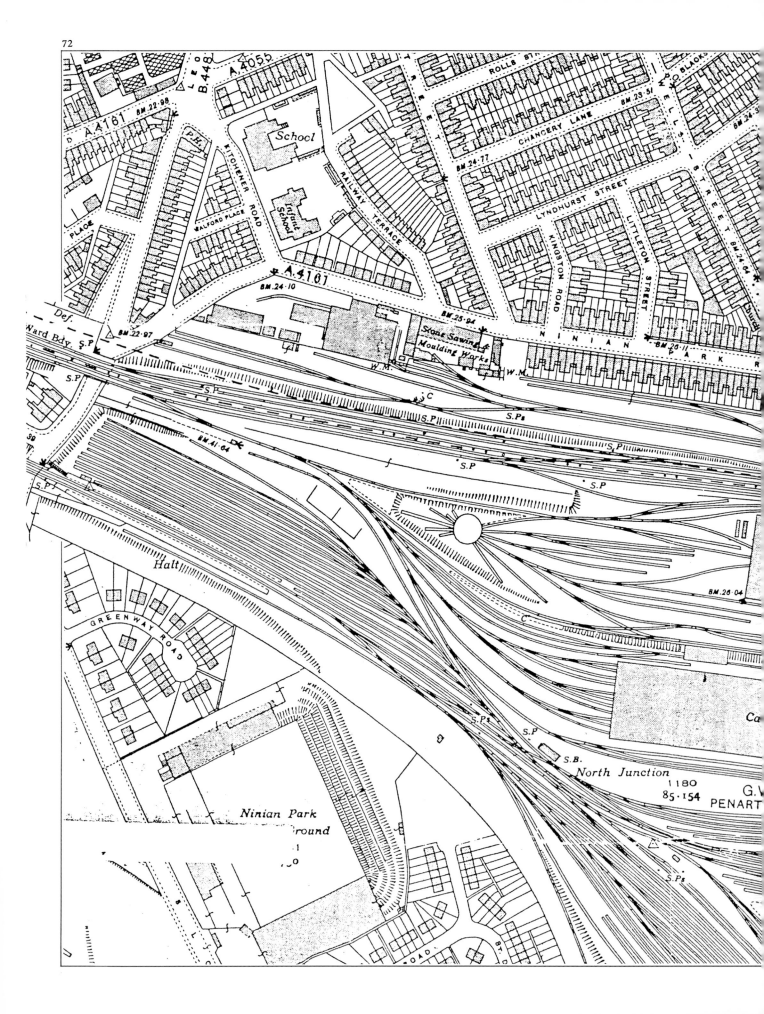

At the end of 1952, the depot received five new 'Britannia' Pacifics, which performed well at the depot, leading to the whole of the Western Region fleet of these engines being based at Canton from 1957.

The introduction of diesel hydraulics in the West Country gradually displaced the 'Kings' from some of their traditional routes, and from September 1960, six were allocated to Canton for the London and Shrewsbury workings. Restrictions that permitted their use only eastwards from Cardiff limited the daily mileage they could run; their short stay at Canton lasted only until 1962, when some were withdrawn and others transferred away as the introduction of diesel hydraulics quickly spread.

Canton was always an important depot for long-distance milk, fish and parcels work, for which the 'high-mileage' passenger engines were used.

In postwar and nationalised years, large numbers of 'Halls', '28XXs' and 'WDs' displaced the previous goods fleets of 'Bulldogs', 'Aberdares', 'RODs' and 'Dean Goods', and this evolution culminated in the depot receiving a large number of double-chimney Standard 'Class 9s' at the end of the 1950s, initially for the Banbury iron ore services, but quickly spreading to all long-distance freight. The depot continued to maintain a large number of tank engines for local shunting and freight work between the South Wales yards.

In order to permit conversion of Canton shed for diesel operation, the surviving steam engines were transferred across to Cardiff East Dock shed in September 1962. East Dock shed was closed in August 1965, although steam services through Cardiff lingered on for a few more weeks.

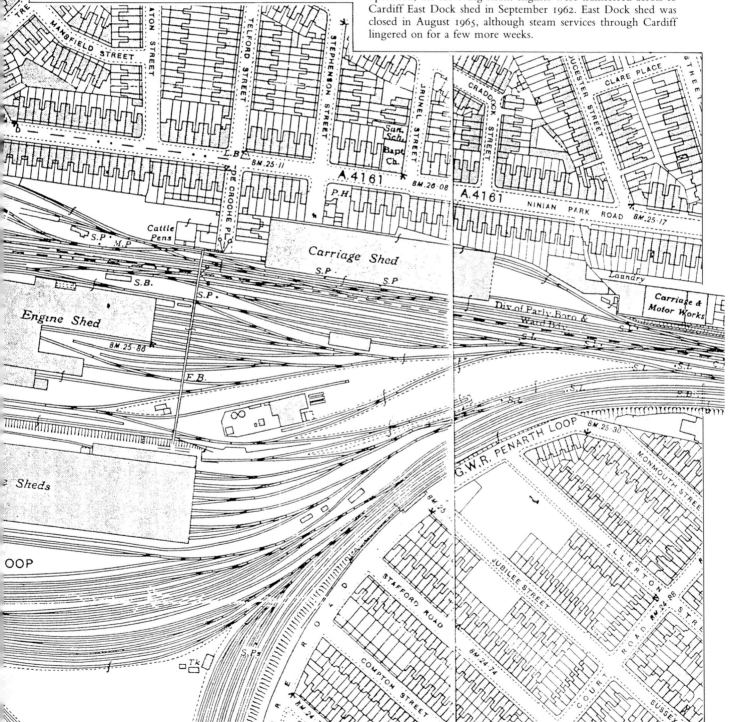

Taken from 25-inch Ordnance Survey for 1942. (Crown copyright reserved)

A Sunday view of Canton 'Castle' No.5099 *Compton Castle*, being prepared for the 4.45 p.m. to Paddington, a relief service preceding the 11.55 a.m. Pembroke Dock. The quality of the coal provided for this engine, for 'Hall' No.7901 *Dodington Hall* (Bath Road shed) and 'County' No.1025 *County of Radnor* (Shrewsbury) can be seen.

With views over the whole of the east end of Canton shed, the footbridge was an excellent vantage point for photographing groups of engines, and movements around the depot. This smoky view, taken in 1959, shows engines raising steam, with Landore 'Castle' No. 4097 *Kenilworth Castle* 'head down' (facing west) for Swansea, and a Canton Standard 'Class 4' awaiting an eastbound turn.

The eastwards access to and from Canton shed is clearly seen in this view of a gleaming 'Britannia', No.70028 *Royal Star*, moving off towards General station on 6th November 1953. The engine had been at Canton for about a year, and was scheduled for the 12.20 p.m. working to Paddington on this occasion. The handrails on its smoke deflectors were later removed. An excellent view is also afforded of the former eastern coaling stage, with its three coaling points, and the inevitable water tank over; by this time, only the stage to the south of the shed was in use. A turntable once stood in the right foreground, but a new one was provided at the west end of the shed site in 1931.

Croes Newydd 'Manors' were not a familiar sight at Canton, though their '28XXs' would often work in. No.7817 *Garsington Manor* was being prepared to work a return trip at Canton on Wednesday, 4th June 1958, 'head up' (facing east) near the footbridge. The engine had received a generous load of coal, and the lid to the water tank was open to receive top-up.

The evening sun casting a strong shadow across Canton's favourite 'Modified Hall' No.6999 *Capel Dewi Hall*. The engine was standing alongside the canteen, waiting to go off shed to work the 5.55 p.m. Paddington to Carmarthen ('The Red Dragon') onwards from General station at 9.15 p.m. to Swansea. The former gas plant can be seen in the background.

In the early 1950s, Canton had two Dean '2301' class 0-6-0s, used mostly on lighter goods duties during the week. On Sundays, they were retained for possible duties over the Severn Bridge on diverted trains between Cardiff and Bristol when the Severn Tunnel was closed. No.2537 is seen here under the southern end of Canton footbridge, with the canteen building to its left. No.2537 was withdrawn from traffic at Canton in January 1953.

Taff Vale '04' class 0-6-2T No.208, attached to the rear of 'Dean' No.2537 at the end of the disposal road, awaiting attention. Canton had several TV class '04s' and 'As' as well as some Barry and Brecon & Merthyr 0-6-2Ts in the early 1950s for local freight and shed pilot duties. The TV and Barry engines had mostly arrived with the closure of Penarth Dock shed in 1929, when several duties around Grangetown and Cardiff performed by that depot were also transferred to Canton.

'Castle' No.5097 *Sarum Castle* (Canton), 'Grange' No.6849 *Walton Grange* (St. Philip's Marsh) and '28XX' class No.3804 (Pontypool Road) alongside the straight-road portion of the shed, with *Evening Star* just inside the shed on the right in early 1961.

In 1960, twelve 'Britannias' remained in Cardiff Canton's allocation, three of which, including Nos.70023 *Venus* and 70022 *Tornado*, are seen in this view. '9F' No.92220, to their left, continued the 'Star' naming sequence of six of the 'Britannias' in carrying 'Evening Star'.

On descending the steps near the southern end of the footbridge, heading towards the foreman's office at Canton, a fine view of the engines assembled outside the east end of the shed could be obtained. Looking across the cabs and fireboxes, 'Kings', a 'Hall' and a Standard 'Class 9' can be seen, with the southern end of the long footbridge ending alongside Canton carriage shed.

Three of the nameplates of Canton's 'Britannias' captured: *Flying Dutchman* (70018), *Tornado* (70022) and *Vulcan* (70024). The batch 70014 to 70029 all carried names of GWR broad gauge or '3001' class engines, twelve of which were at Canton. Originally, the 'Britannias' had handrails across their smoke deflectors, but, apparently following an incident in which difficulties in 'sighting' (caused by the position of the handrail) were involved, they were replaced by cut-outs, as seen here.

On most visits to the shed, there were imposing views of at least one of the 'Britannias'. Here, No.70027 *Rising Star* was awaiting the 1.0 p.m. duty to London (train No.A64) in the summer of 1960.

One of the 'higher mileage' Britannias' at the time, No.70029 *Shooting Star*, facing 'head down' on Canton shed in readiness for a westbound duty. The engine would no doubt have taken over an express or class '3' ('C') to Swansea, where the demands on steaming and timekeeping were somewhat less than that experienced on the run to and from Paddington, which were generally the preserve of the shed's ex-works 'low mileage' engines. Canton's later shed code '88A' (from early 1961) is clearly discernible, a number that was transferred along with the engines to Cardiff East Dock in 1962. '88A' code formerly identified Cathays and Radyr, which subsequently became '88M' (diesel) and '88B' respectively.

How the Canton shine was achieved – a cleaning gang giving their attention to 'Castle' No.7020 *Gloucester Castle* outside the straight-road shed at the east end of Canton in the early 1950s. The huge pile of coal on the tender would probably have been out of gauge until levelled by the fireman, prior to working the engine to Paddington.

The prototype 'Castle' – No.4073 *Caerphilly Castle* – standing under Canton footbridge in readiness for her next working to Paddington. The train number '747' was used in the mid-1950s to signify the second part of the 12.0 noon Milford Haven to Paddington when run as three trains, and was formed by the stock of the 11.20 a.m. Pembroke Dock running forward as the 12.46 p.m. from Whitland. The first part (746) came from Treherbert and Blaina (both via Bassaleg Jet. and Newport), whilst the main train (745) ran third in the sequence. No.4073 spent virtually all of its GWR career at Old Oak, though it was shedded at Canton for a few months in 1935, following which it moved to Landore for a couple more. No.4073 was moved to Bath Road in 1950, and back to Canton in February 1957, where she stayed until withdrawn from traffic in 1960, pending preservation at South Kensington.

Canton's Standard Class '5' 4-6-0 No.73025 on shed on 26th January 1957, a photograph taken on the first day that I used my first 35mm camera, a Voigtlander Vito II. Four of the engines were allocated to Canton at this time, and when ex-works got a few runs to Salisbury on the top 'Hall' turn, though they soon gravitated onto the Saltney freights, along with similar Chester engines. When scheduled for regular freight turns, they soon lost their Canton shine, as cleaning efforts were more usually directed at the passenger engines.

A view of engines standing outside the east end of Canton, looking west at the straight-road shed buildings in April 1960. 'County' No.1011 *County of Chester* (from Bath Road) was scheduled for the 12.32 p.m. to Bristol, whilst the 'Castle' carrying train No.953 was destined for the 1.13 p.m. Cardiff (11.50 a.m. Swansea) to Manchester (Piccadilly). The recently-acquired 'Castle', 5021 *Whittington Castle*, at the front had arrived from Laira shed the previous September, with a 'Class 9' to its right.

Although Canton housed many 4-6-0s, there were also a number of 2-8-0 and 2-10-0 engines for freight duties to such destinations as Bristol, Saltney, Hackney Sdgs, Tavistock Jet, Acton, Banbury and Woodford (ex-GCR). 'WD' (8F) No.90572 is seen here on the sidings alongside the 'northlight' pattern straight-road shed next to Swindon 'County' No.1019 *County of Merioneth* on Sunday, 22nd September 1957.

A contrast in latter-day motive power for South Wales services. 'King' No.6028 *King George VI*, with steam to spare, at the straight-road shed at Canton with 'Britannia' No.70022 *Tornado*. The headboard on the 'King' was for the 7.20 p.m. mail to Pontypool Road, whilst No.70022 was 'head down' and probably waiting for the 5.45 p.m. down (10.35 a.m. Kensington) milk empties.

Bath Road 'County' No.1009 *County of Carmarthen* alongside Standard Class '4' 4-6-0 No.75022; Canton had around six of the latter engines, which were similar to the Class '5s' ('73XXXs') in outline, but with smaller wheels. Operationally, the Class '4s' were similar to the 'Manor' class, with the same 'Blue' route availability and loading. The extreme left of this picture just features No.90565. The view here shows the south-facing wall of the straight-road shed, the road nearest to which provided exit from the roundhouse portion of Canton.

Initially, the 'Counties' were to be seen only on the 'Double Red' routes cleared for the 'King' class locomotives, but they were soon officially cleared onwards to Swansea, via Badminton (with speed restrictions in South Wales, particularly the 40 mph over the Skewen viaduct) by the Chief Engineer in May 1946. As early as August 1946, Old Oak 'Counties' were noted on Cardiff trains, and in October of that year were seen regularly on such services as the 3·55 p.m. Paddington and the 8.15 p.m. Neyland trains. In October 1948, three of the class were allocated to Neyland, and worked up to Cardiff, normally on class 'C' trains. From the east, the Bath Road and Swindon engines were a familiar sight at Cardiff. No.1023 *County of Oxford* was transferred from Exeter to Swindon shed in 1961, and is seen here awaiting its next duty, the 11.0 a.m. Swansea to Penzance, due out of Cardiff at 12.32 p.m.

The south side of the straight road shed at Canton on 30th July 1958, with the two entrances to the roundhouse section in the background to the left. During 1958-60, a stream of new, double-chimney Standard class '9F' 2-10-os emerged from Swindon works, and each visit to Canton would see a new example on display. No.92229 was a recent addition to the scene, sitting back-to-back with its Great Western counterpart, the '28XX'.

'Britannia' No.70024 *Vulcan*, illustrating the degree of external pipework not present on ex-GWR designs. In operating terms, the 'Britannias' were subject to the same route and load restrictions as the 'Castles', being in the 'Red' group. This engine had an extended period of London workings to see what an ex-works 'Britannia' was capable of, in which it was doubtless compared with the recently transferred 'Kings', and perhaps with the Great Eastern section 'Britannias'. No.70024 is seen here in the spring of 1961, in its usual immaculate condition, awaiting yet another turn to Paddington.

A left-hand side view of No.70028 *Royal Star*, one of the original five engines sent new to Canton in the latter half of 1952, standing outside the straight-road shed at Canton. The group of staff were enjoying the fresh air and sunshine outside the grime of the shed.

A panoramic, if somewhat smoky, view of Canton shed from the east, taken from the top of the water tower on top of the former coaling plant on 8th September 1962, just before the closure of the shed. After rebuilding work, Canton reopened as a diesel depot. Canton carriage shed is on the extreme left-hand edge of the picture, with the lights of Ninian Park football ground towering over the far end. The centre of the picture illustrates the shed, with the stores building to the left and the straight road shed in the centre, largely obscured by smoke. Canton Sidings box is clearly visible towards the right-hand edge of the picture, with the main and relief running lines to its right, and the mileage yard beyond. From the left, 'Grange' No.6833 *Calcot Grange*, 'Hall' No.5961 *Toynbee Hall*, 'County' No.1009 *County of Carmarthen* and an unidentified 'Castle' can be seen in a largely-abandoned shed, the move to East Dock being well under way.

Portrait of a 'King' – No.6004 *King George III* was transferred at Canton in September 1960, though it returned to Old Oak in the following year. The engine passing the 'stores' building on her way from the coal stage, was about to work the 12 noon from Cardiff General station (8.0 a.m. Neyland) to Paddington on Saturday, 24th September 1960, carrying the appropriate 'A58' train identification board. She was being watched by Charlie Hewlett, the shift foreman.

A view of the south-eastern corner of Canton shed, looking west. On the left of the picture is the repair shop, with the stores building to its right, in the centre of the picture. The roundhouse was located behind the latter structure; locomotives entered it from the west end, and left by means of two roads that passed between the stores and the straight road shed (with its distinctive northlight pattern roof) on the right. Amongst the engines on view in this photograph, taken on 2nd November 1957, are 'Hall' No.6944 *Fledborough Hall* (Shrewsbury), '28XX' No.3810 (Canton) and 'Halls' Nos.7927 *Willington Hall* (Reading) and 5977 *Beckford Hall* (Hereford).

The disposal road at Canton led down to the coal stage at the southern end of the shed. Fires were dropped, tubes were cleaned, and many other filthy tasks associated with the maintenance of steam engines were carried out there, and the bank alongside was an excellent location from which to photograph parked engines. Llanelly's Class '5' No.73021 is shown standing on the road awaiting attention, still with a good load of coal in the tender; it would probably only have required fire cleaning and some water before returning west. The '73XXX' class 4-6-0s were given the same 'Red' route availability and a similar loading to the 'Halls'. The shed pilot, No.1508, can be seen beyond the tender, and a '94XX' 0-6-0T and at the near end. WD No.90573, in front of the stores building, had recently returned ex-works.

A view looking eastwards along the southern side of the shed from a coaling platform, with the remainder of the coaling stage on the right and the disposal road beyond. It offers an unusual view, normally only seen by members of the coaling gang. The repair shop is on the left, with the through shed road running in front of it, and the long footbridge serving the carriage shed in the distance. The middle siding between the through and disposal roads had been all but buried, with only the turnout and the occasional glimpse of rail to mark its course. The first locomotive on the disposal road was Canton's 'Manor' No.7820 *Dinmore Manor*, which was next for coaling. It had probably already had its fire attended to (or dropped), and, after coaling, would have been turned and probably taken back to the east end to await its next turn. If no duty had been assigned, the locomotive may well have remained at the west end of the shed.

The now preserved Old Oak 'Castle' No.5029 *Nunney Castle* on the coal stage road, off the south-western corner of the shed. One of the coaling points had been extended over the adjacent through line, to give more flexibility in coaling operations. The sidings contained many double-chimney class '9F' freight engines, and an example of the once-numerous ex-LMS '4F' 0-6-0s. No.44203; from Saltley shed, Birmingham.

A portrait of '43XX' class 2-6-0 No.5378, from Tyseley shed, on the disposal road in 1961, with the repair shop in the background. These engines were still frequent visitors at this time, and another of the class can be seen alongside. Canton itself had No.6326 in its allocation during 1961. The '42XX' 2-8-0T was also awaiting attention.

A fully-coaled 'Grange' 4-6-0 No.6812 *Chesford Grange* from Pontypool Road shed outside the repair shop on the southern side of the shed, c.1959. The engine was standing on the siding between the disposal and through roads, normally used for engines that required coal (or had been coaled) but no further servicing, thus avoiding the queue of locomotives requiring full attention in the busy disposal road. No.6812 had been coaled and turned, and was awaiting movement to the east end of the shed.

Standard '9F' 2-10-0 No.92222 is seen standing on the siding alongside the disposal road, behind the 'Grange', c.1959. The south-western corner of the roundhouse can be seen beyond, with No.90691 standing on the adjacent repair shop road. In the distance, on the sidings to the west of the roundhouse shed, we can see examples of '56XX', '28XX' and '94XX' classes.

A feature of Canton shed was the use of a shed pilot, which always remained within the confines of the depot. Duties included servicing the coal stage with loaded wagons and removing empties, which were taken across to Penarth Curve yard, behind the carriage shed. It also serviced the stores with wagons of materials, moved dead engines around the yard, and performed any other movements required. The final engine provided for this duty was the '15XX' class o-6-oT No.1508, which was transferred from Severn Tunnel Jct. for the purpose in 1956, though this was probably not the sort of work Swindon envisaged for these powerful shunting locomotives. The west end of Canton roundhouse, seen behind the engine, was served from three entrances. In this view, the pilot was moving an ex-Caerphilly works '16XX' class engine and some wagons onto the stop-block road.

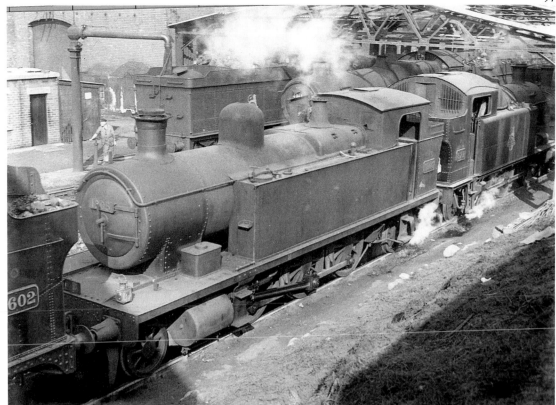

Another shed pilot of the 1950s was the ex-Alexandra Docks & Railway 2-6-2T No.1205, which was transferred from Llantrisant to Canton around 1950, and remained until withdrawn in January 1956. A Hawthorn, Leslie engine, No.1205 was the last AD & R locomotive in British Railways service.

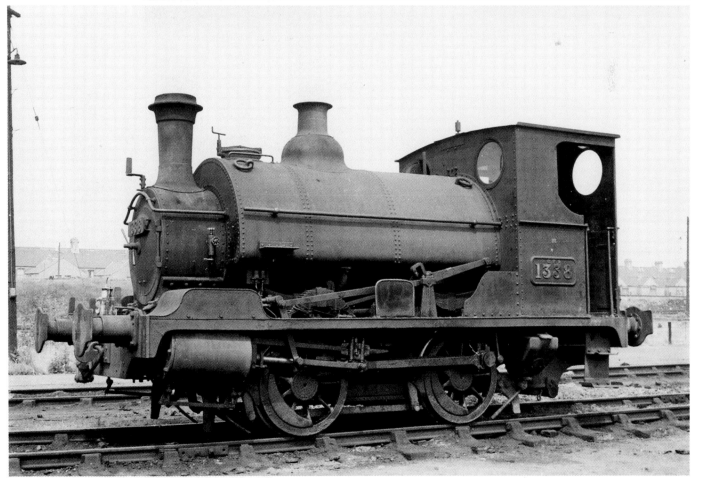

Ex-Cardiff Railway Kitson 0-4-0ST No.1338, seen here in the loco yard at Canton. This engine dated from 1898, and survived until 1963, when it was sold for preservation. No.1338 came to Canton from Taunton (for Bridgwater Docks) for a short time after the withdrawal of No.1205, but was required for further shunting duties at Taunton/Bridgwater, so her presence was enjoyed for only a short time.

In 1931, a new 65ft turntable was installed at Canton, on the extreme west end of the shed yard. 'County' No.1022 *County of Northampton* (Shrewsbury) is seen on the table on 31st January 1959. The sidings above the turntable containing loco coal wagons (which were unloaded onto a stack) were late additions to the yard, constructed some time after the 1934 rebuilding scheme, but before 1950.

The end of an era. The west yard of Canton yard, deserted except for No.1508 on pilot duties, September 1962. The coal stage road is in the foreground, with a good view of the extended coaling point onto the adjacent road. The diesel shed was rebuilt on the same site as the steam depot, with servicing and maintenance structures positioned alongside each other.

Canton 'Hall' class 4-6-0 No.6939 *Calveley Hall* accelerating away past Canton with the 9.25 a.m. Manchester (London Road) to Swansea express on Wednesday, 30th July 1958. The engine took the Manchester train on from Cardiff for the 80-minute journey to Swansea, then returned with the 6.52 p.m. Swansea to Bristol semi-fast ('B' lamp) passenger as far as Cardiff. After running back to Canton, the engine picked up the 5.20 p.m. Milford Haven fish, which it hauled to Swindon, returning from Marston Sidings to Cardiff with milk empties for Whitland. These duties illustrate the variety of different trains that could be worked within the course of a turn by these engines.

In September 1962, Canton shed was closed to steam locomotives. The survivors were transferred across to Cardiff East Dock shed, located at the very centre of the dock complex, outside Stonefield Jct signal box. In the foreground, the fires of '43XX' 2-6-0 No.6357 and a '72XX' class 2-8-2T were receiving attention on the coal road, whilst No.5092 *Tresco Abbey* was moving off shed to run as far as Long Dyke, whence she would reverse past Newtown goods shed, through 'the General' station and on to the carriage shed at Canton to pick up her train.

Photographs by R. O. Tuck appear on the following pages: Preface, opposite page 1, 1, 2 (top & bottom), 3 (top & bottom), 4 (top & bottom), 5, 6 (middle & bottom), 7 (top & bottom), 9 (top & bottom), 11, 12, 16, 18, 20 (top), 23 (top & bottom), 25 (top), 27, 29, 37 (bottom), 43, 47 (bottom), 64, 75 (bottom), 90 (top & bottom), 91 (top) and 99 (top).